Lyle's Administration of the College Library

1997 Text Edition

Caroline M. Coughlin
and
Alice Gertzog

The Scarecrow Press, Inc.
Lanham, Md., & London
1997

SCARECROW PRESS, INC.

Published in the United States of America
by Scarecrow Press, Inc.
4720 Boston Way
Lanham, Maryland 20706

4 Pleydell Gardens, Folkestone
Kent CT20 2DN, England

British Library Cataloguing in Publication Information Available

Library of Congress Cataloging-in-Publication Data

Coughlin, Caroline M.
    Lyle's administration of the college library / Caroline M. Coughlin and Alice
Gertzog. — 1997 text ed.
        p.   cm.
    Based on Lyle's administration of the college library. 5th ed. 1992.
    Includes bibliographical references and index.
    ISBN 0-8108-3333-6 (alk. paper). — ISBN 0-8108-3330-1 (pbk. : alk. paper)
    1. Academic libraries—United States—Administration. I. Gertzog,   Alice. I.
Title.
    Z675.U5C767   1997
    025.1'977—dc21   97-8758

ISBN 0-8108-3333-6 (cloth : alk. paper)
ISBN 0-8108-3330-1 (pbk. : alk. paper)

♾™ The paper used in this publication meets the minimum requirements of
American National Standard for Information Sciences—Permanence of
Paper for Printed Library Materials, ANSI Z39.48–1984.
Manufactured in the United States of America.

Dedicated
to
Guy Redvers Lyle
1907 - 1994
An author of uncommon wisdom

CONTENTS

FIGURES

PREFACE TO THE TEXT EDITION

The authors of the text edition, also the authors of the fifth edition, are aware of the historic importance of the earlier editions of *The Administration of the College Library* by Guy R. Lyle and eager to continue the tradition of offering those interested in academic librarianship an overview of all relevant topics. For these reasons we authored the fifth edition, published by Scarecrow Press in 1992. That volume, all 603 pages of it, was welcomed as a valuable edition to the literature of academic librarianship. However, its very size (and price) made it difficult to use as a text in classes in library science. Since that audience is an important one to us, we have chosen to modify the material in the fifth edition and create a text edition. In this volume you will find the material in chapters 1 through 6 of the library edition virtually unchanged except for some modest updating of statistics. Four other chapters on user services, library staff, planning and evaluation issues focus on the policy segments of the related chapters in the fifth edition. Technological concerns are identified although examples of particular technological applications are limited. The Appendix is the newest version of the *Standards for College Libraries.*

We are grateful to our families for their continued support and to Dean Jon Oliver and the staff of the Computer Laboratory at the School of Communication, Information and Library Studies at Rutgers University who were invaluable sources of technical advice throughout the creation of this edition.

As authors of both editions we hope that each finds its reader. To the students using this text edition we offer a welcome to the challenge of making academic librarianship the profession it can be, full of intellectual vigor and creativity, a field that offers opportunities to bring new knowledge to the tasks of higher education.

PREFACE TO THE FIFTH EDITION

This is the fifth edition of *Lyle's Administration of the College Library*. The fourth edition appeared in 1974 and the first in 1944.

When Alphonse Karr wrote in 1849, "the more things change, the more they are the same," he could hardly have envisioned the rapid rate of global movement, shift, and development occurring almost daily in the last decade of the twentieth century. Yet his aphorism is no less true today than when he framed it, particularly as it applies to libraries. Librarians do what they have always done. They organize information.

Still, comparing this fifth edition with Lyle's first exploration into the world of college library administration almost a half a century ago reveals how substantially library practices have changed in the intervening period. New technology, electronic publishing, systems approaches, planning techniques, network development, increased understanding of environmental, societal, and political forces, and user behavior and information needs account for the major differences between the first edition and the fifth.

Lyle set out to write a simple, logical, and self-contained introduction to "all aspects of library administration as they applied to college libraries." Our aim is the same. Lyle hoped that his book would be helpful to library school students and librarians new to their positions in academic libraries. We wish for no less. We have tried also to emulate Lyle's middle-ground approach to the subject—neither purely philosophical nor totally experiential, a broad view with a practical component. Lyle's success was legendary. Indeed, an informal survey we administered when writing this text revealed that many library school classes were still using the 1974 edition as a primary text in 1990.

The authors are grateful to Guy R. Lyle for his permission to produce a new edition. His remarkable accomplishment served as model, challenge and motivating force for us throughout the process of creating this work.

The structure of the current edition, while bearing a strong resemblance to Lyle's now reflects an increased contextual and systems framework. New chapters on technology, the library director, a campus inventory, and bibliographic instruction have been added, and Lyle's chapters on the educational function and encouraging the reading habit have been integrated into other parts of the book. When library practices are unchanged, Lyle's words remain as he wrote them.

Permission to reprint the *Standards for College Libraries* was granted by the American Library Association.

In the preparation of chapters, the staff of the Drew University and Allegheny College Libraries lent invaluable support and assistance. Particular thanks are due to Jean Schoenthaler, Alice Copeland, Pam Snelson, Evelyn Meyer, Jan Wanggaard, Eleanor Rawitz, Stacy Moseman, Bruce Lancaster, and Josepha Cook of Drew University, and Helen McCullough, Cynthia Burton, and Don Vrabel of Allegheny College. Valerie Weinberg and Barbara Kwasnik counseled us about the cataloging chapter. Andrew Ford, Provost of Allegheny College, increased our understanding of factors to be considered in inventorying a college campus. Mary Jo Lynch served as a resource about college library statistics. Judy Weinberg translated sketches into usable graphics. The Oberlin Group of College Library Directors shared their experiences with us in an informative questionnaire and in personal contacts. Tom Limoncelli, Dottie Friedman, and Ellen Falduto assisted us with preparation of the manuscript. We are grateful to them all.

Will and Nora Weinberg and Irwin Gertzog, while patiently awaiting completion of the project, supplied support, meals, comfort, and distraction. To them we dedicate this book with our sincerest thanks.

Chapter 1

CONTEXTS OF THE AMERICAN COLLEGE LIBRARY

College librarians, to quote the old Chinese curse, are certainly living in interesting times. They face a fluid and uncertain environment shaped primarily by technological advances and demographic changes as well as by diminished resources and new demands on their profession. Developments in software, equipment, and materials occur at a dizzying pace. Keeping up is difficult.

Librarians are commanded to be aggressive, to assume a greater teaching role, to be collegial, to guard against producing a generation of information have-nots, to be more accountable, to manage with fewer dollars, and to offer new services. At the same time, librarians are also expected to protect and purvey traditional humanistic values, to bear responsibility for preserving cultural artifacts, to create information-literate students, and to champion reading as the essential skill of an educated person.

Some librarians contend that technology only provides new and speedier ways to do what libraries have always done. Others maintain that technology has so changed the nature of information that even the basic processes now differ. Both arguments have merit. People still ask questions. Librarians still help them find answers. But new words have entered the vocabulary. For instance, we are as likely to talk about "access" as we are about "acquisition." The traditional description of roles played by a library—to acquire, organize, and disseminate information—now require far broader definitions of acquisition and dissemination than once characterized the concepts. Moreover, new responsibilities have been promoted by technology. The emergence of the wired campus, which enables students as well as faculty to interface directly with the library without a human mediator, mandates that librarians find ways to intervene in the information process. They must teach their constituencies about the nature, use, and evaluation of information. It is no longer sufficient to introduce students to the library as part of a first-year orientation program. The task, rather, is to make users information-literate, no matter how or where they gain access to information.

William Moffett considered a college to be a mostly undergraduate institution with less than four thousand students and with libraries containing no more than one million volumes.[1] That definition describes most of the libraries for which the information contained in this volume will be useful. However, distinctions applied on the basis of size of student population are of lesser importance. Though college libraries share the umbrella term "academic" with those in universities, they exhibit as many differences from university libraries as they do similarities. For instance, college libraries are often seen as the last refuge of "generalists," while university libraries provide comfortable environments for "specialists." College librarians like to consider themselves Renaissance people; those in universities strive for depth and disciplinary comprehensiveness.

Colleges focus on teaching first and place research second. Nonetheless, they differ in their missions. Some are oriented toward the liberal arts, others toward vocational training. Some boast that their curriculum contains no courses of "practice"; others brag that their curriculum prepares students for a job. Neither assertion accurately describes any college. All courses can be placed on a continuum as more or less practical in orientation. College libraries, too, can be seen as existing on a continuum with collections ranging from extensive and deep in elite, private liberal arts institutions to minimal, albeit occasionally excellent, collections in newer schools, or colleges with less money, or colleges where the stress is less on library usage and more on text learning. No matter the nature of the institution or the library, its fundamental activities and concerns remain similar. Methods may differ in particular libraries, but the major functions are basically alike. Successful techniques do not vary greatly from one library to another.

ENVIRONMENTS

The purpose of this book is to describe the work involved in administering a college library. All college libraries are products of and are influenced by factors external to the campus; the social structure of the college; the internal configuration of the library; and the nature of the relationships between these elements and how they interact.

Therefore, successful administration of a contemporary college library requires an understanding not only of how to run the library, but of the larger context in which the library functions. Academic library service, its provision, and use occur in, are affected by, and affect what happens in the library's its immediate and greater environment.

Prior to the 1970s, academic librarians assumed that their libraries occupied a relatively stable place in their relatively stable institutions in a slowly changing library world. Accordingly, they concentrated most of their efforts on improving the efficiency of internal functions and tended to ignore how forces outside their institutions affected them. They were also inclined to downplay the importance of campus political and social relationships. The 1980s produced a sea change in attitudes toward knowledge and information, and in the delivery of library services. These changes, coupled with the accelerated pace of social ferment, technological development, and the application of systems theories to social organizations, ended forever any notion that libraries were independent of their environments. The myth of the self-sufficient college library had been shattered.

Five environments can be considered to surround a college library. Each of these environments is described below and is accompanied by an example that illustrates how one event may produce a ripple effect and influence can be exerted or experienced. Figure 1 represents the way in which a college library is embedded within multiple environments.

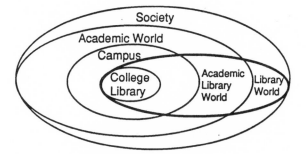

Contexts of a College Library

The *society,* which encompasses social, economic, political, and cultural trends. Among these may be public attitudes toward education and society's assessments of the importance of information. The baby boomlet of 1984 will affect the number and quality of students who will attend college in 2002, and this, in turn, will have an impact on the demand for library services.

The *academic world,* which includes, among other elements, the current state of knowledge, research agendas, faculty supply and demand, curriculum priorities, pedagogical and governance trends, and financial support. The curriculum reform movement of the late 1980s has major importance for collection development decisions.

The *library world*, which is comprised of the sectors of practice, scholarship, and those agencies that serve the profession, as, for instance, library associations and the organs of communication, library periodicals. The degree to which the profession is currently successful in promoting librarianship as a challenging and rewarding career will influence a college library's ability to recruit a capable staff in the immediate future.

The a*cademic library world,* which includes methods and practices, both new and traditional, for the provision of efficient and effective college and university library service. The development of bibliographic instruction methods that utilize a problem-solving/ decision-making approach will change the manner in which College Library X introduces students to in-house library research.

The *college community*, the most direct context in which a library operates, includes the faculty, students, and administration. It has a social structure produced by, among other factors, its history, traditions, geography, cultural climate, resources, size, and academic quality and orientation. Lack of success in recruiting a sufficient number of tuition-paying students by the administration of College X may result in reduced resources for the library.

SYSTEMS THEORY

Daily, librarians, and indeed college faculty and administrators concerned with the library, are faced with myriad questions about the extent to which the library is meeting its purpose or potential. Mere facts do not supply answers. Knowing, for instance, that more than 50 percent of all college students use the library only four hours or less a week says little about whether that is an adequate or insufficient amount.[2] Studying the issue in context may help. In recent years, systems theory has been widely applied to help describe and explain the workings of libraries. This approach is useful because it assumes that the elements and structures of the institution should be thought of as parts of a whole and as they affect one another rather than as distinct entities to be examined separately. Some generalizations about systems theory follow:

1. Systems are composed of interrelated parts and elements;
2. They are not merely the sum of parts, but a totality and should be viewed holistically;
3. Systems are relatively open or closed based on the extent to which they exchange information, energy or material with their environments;
4. They are more or less bounded and separated from their environments;
5. Systems are characterized by inputs and throughputs, as well as by outputs, which in turn provide feedback and appear as future inputs;
6. They are comprised of subsystems and are part of suprasystems;
7. Systems generally achieve something. In other words, they are organized for a particular purpose.[3]

Libraries are relatively open systems that depend on their environment for inputs and for feedback. They both draw from and contribute to their environments in order to meet social expectations. A systems model (figure 2), based on one devised by Joanne Euster,[4] utilizes a two-environment approach to describe the dynamics of an academic library.

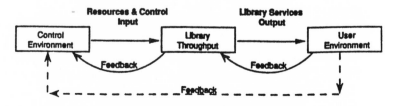

Campus Environments: A Systems Model

The *control* environment provides the input—the resources and controls on which the library depends for survival—and evaluates the goals, methods, and outputs. Inputs are generally considered to be money, services, personnel, and information. Among the controls are the degree of autonomy granted the library. This includes its ability to define or alter its mission, goals, and scope of activities, and its freedom to devise methods to meet its goals and conduct its program.

The *user* environment refers to all segments of the college community that receive the services of the library—the outputs—including students, faculty, administration, and those in the wider library community and in the local geographic community who are served by the college library. Outputs may be considered in terms of measurable activities and operations, including circulation, in-house library use, assistance in the use of the library ,and answers to reference questions. Alternatively, outputs may refer to changes in library patrons as a result of library use.[5]

Feedback in this model is delivered directly to the library from its user environment and from the library to its control environment. Feedback from the user environment flows weakly to the control environment. User and control environments in an academic community share personnel who play different roles in each setting. Administrators, for instance, are members of the control environment but function, at times, as library service consumers.

The *library* is the place where the elements and activities are transformed from energy and information (inputs) into exportable products (outputs). Elements used in the process are the collection and its surrogate, the catalog. The activities usually involved in the conversion are technical processes—acquisitions, cataloging, classification and collection maintenance; public services—circulation, reference services, readers advisory services; administration—planning, organizing, motivating and controlling.[6]

Figure 3 illustrates the internal process of converting energy and information (inputs) into usable library products (outputs).

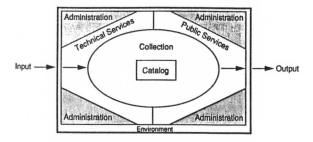

The Library System

Of these activities, some are more boundary spanning, that is, they are located closer to the system's borders than others. Cataloging, for instance, has traditionally been relatively remote from the library's clientele, although it has open boundaries with book dealers, jobbers, and bibliographic networks, among others in the library world. Public services, on the other hand, directly mediate with library users, and library administrators continually confer and negotiate with the control environment. Technological developments have resulted in the need for far greater numbers of public service librarians, people who must deal directly with members of their campus environments, and for many fewer catalogers.

Libraries, like other organizations, react to the environment in two ways. First, they adapt the library to it. Second, they change the environment so that internal adaptation becomes unnecessary. A library wishing to enhance its input, for instance, must change the value of its output either through improved internal processes or through manipulation of the environment's perception of its value.

CHAPTER HIGHLIGHTS

The chapters that follow are organized according to the contextual framework described above. The initial section, chapters 2 through 5, is devoted to the external environments that exert a direct influence on the college library. Chapter 2 describes the growth of higher education in the United States against a background of historic events that bear on its development, traces curriculum reform from its beginnings to the present, and looks at some of the problems in contemporary society and their potential impact on higher education. Chapter 3 explores the history and current condition of academic libraries and librarianship within the framework of their relationship to higher education and their connections to the library world. Chapters 4, 5, and 6 deal with the campus context. Chapter 4 highlights elements which, when joined, describe a unique college. Utilizing an inventory format, dozens of questions are posed about such aspects of campus life as the nature of the student body, the faculty, the administration, trustees, and the curriculum. Chapter 5 describes the legal basis of a college and its governance, as well as its informal political culture. Chapter 6 places the college library within the organizational context of the institution and describes how the library structures itself internally in order to operate. Organizing principles and practices—traditional and new, formal and informal—are presented. For the most part, except for some modest updating of statistical sources, these chapters are reproduced from the library edition of _Lyle's Administration of the College Library_ (5th edition). Chapters 7, 8, 9, and 10 present material from chapters 8 through 20 of the library edition in condensed form. Each now focuses on the policy issues germane to library science students studying the principles of user services, library staffing, planning issues, and evaluation in academic libraries.

SUMMARY

Academic libraries are deeply embedded in a variety of environments, all of which influence the services they provide. Understanding academic libraries as open systems with environmental inputs, boundary-spanning activities, outputs, and feedback mechanisms furnishes librarians with a framework in which to examine what they do and with whom they do it. Ultimately, this understanding permits them to exercise greater flexibility and more control over their circumstances. Systems theory will give an integrated overview of how an academic library works. However, it is not the only method of analysis used by directors, and it must always be combined with intimate knowledge of an institution's particular framework.

NOTES

1. William Moffett, "Reflections of a College Librarian," _College and Research Libraries_ 45, (May 1984): 338.

2. Patricia Breivik and Robert Wedgeworth, *Libraries and the Search for Academic Excellence* (Metuchen, N.J.: Scarecrow Press, 1988), 7.

3. Freemont E. Kast and James Rosenzweig, "General Systems Theory," in *Management Strategies for Libraries*, ed. Beverly Lynch (New York: Neal-Schuman, 1985), 132.

4. Joanne Euster, *Activities and Effectiveness of the Academic Library Director* (Westport, Conn.: Greenwood Press, 1987), 36.

5. Maurice Marchant, "The Library as Open System," in *Management Strategies for Libraries,* ed. Beverly Lynch (New York: Neal-Schuman, 1985), 154-56.

6. Marchant, *Management Strategies*, 153.

Chapter 2

EVOLUTION OF HIGHER EDUCATION IN THE UNITED STATES

Higher education in the United States today, as in the past, is an outgrowth of social trends and national needs and policies. Just as college libraries reflect the changing priorities of their parent institutions, colleges themselves mirror values extant in the society at a particular time. While the times prepare the way for change, no social movement or organization is successful without strong leaders who help to shape and further it. Higher education today is a product of the earlier efforts of many distinguished pioneers. Charles W. Eliot of Harvard, Mary Lyons of Mt. Holyoke, Senator Samuel Morrill of Vermont, Daniel Coit Gilman of Johns Hopkins, George Washington Carver of Tuskeegee ,and Robert Hutchins of the University of Chicago were all significant contributors to the rich mosaic of higher education. Their names are associated, respectively, with the growth of elective curricula, making higher education available to women, sponsoring legislation to establish land grant colleges, establishing research as a priority of education, providing educational opportunities to former slaves, and developing methodologies to improve undergraduate education.

COLONIAL COLLEGES

The roots of American higher education lie in the colonial period when numerous colleges were formed primarily to train young men for the ministry. The first college, Harvard, was established in 1636 by the Puritans. The College of William and Mary followed in 1693. Other early institutions included Yale, the College of New Jersey (now Princeton), King's College (now Columbia), Queen's College (Rutgers), the College of Rhode Island (now Brown), The University of Pennsylvania and Dartmouth. With the exception of Columbia and the University of Pennsylvania, all had a religious affiliation. In addition, all were patterned after the English college; that is, they provided a classical education. The task of the early colleges was to educate Christian gentlemen. Their classical curriculum consisted of a formal, almost ritual, series of exercises designed to form the whole man. Classical education was predicated on two important assumptions:

1. Human history and thought are cumulative and progressive. Homer's language, for instance, is simpler than Shakespeare's because it dates from an earlier time.
2. The material of education—what is studied—is less important than its effect in improving the student's mind. The highest function of education is to lay the foundation for further learning.

As a result, the curriculum of a classical college followed a specific historical path, what has been called "a ritualized progression from the Greek historians through the wilderness of mathematics and the natural sciences to reach the abode of the moral philosophers."[1] Memorization and examination were the principal learning devices. Lectures were repeated year after year, particularly as enrollments increased and books were in short supply. The curriculum allowed for no divergent views but rather presented a unified picture of a world without contradiction. Moreover, the quality of a teacher was gauged more by his fealty to religion and the depth of his conviction than by his scholarship. Indeed, scholarship was rejected as an inappropriate undertaking for faculty; they were expected to have learned everything there was to know by the time they began to teach; further education would only have been redundant.

All of the colonial colleges considered themselves private and responsible for their own policy formation, even those that accepted public funds. But they were not self-governing, as their English counterparts had been. Boards of governors or overseers—magistrates, clergy and others—established policy. Presidents, more often than not, handled all disciplinary problems and carried a major teaching load.

In the process of developing a supply of educated Protestant ministers, each of the nine early colleges assumed a position of leadership in the geographic area surrounding it and in the nation. As the country expanded, these institutions supplied men who were instrumental to national growth and development. Other educational institutions, the emerging professions, various social movements, state and federal governments, and, of course, organized religion profited from the dedication of those who had been classically trained in the early colonial colleges.

In the first fifty years of the post-colonial period, the population of the United States quadrupled. The settling of the interior brought with it an increasing demand for additional ministers and resulted in the rapid establishment of colleges by religious denominations in the new communities. State universities, too, were organized. Georgia had one in 1785 and North Carolina in 1789. By 1830, nine states had public academic institutions, and the more than fifty colleges were educating about five thousand male students.

MIDDLE YEARS

The years spanning the crucial Civil War period were marked by diversification, population growth, urbanization, and industrialization. During this time, new institutions of higher education mushroomed throughout the nation. Innovative models of colleges, different from the men's four-year liberal arts institutions, arose as attempts were made to service particular clienteles. Women's colleges were one early variation, ushered in with the establishment of Mount Holyoke in 1836. Oberlin became the first coeducational, multiracial college in the nation when it admitted women and blacks in the late 1830s. Fisk was chartered in 1866. Howard and Morehouse started a year later. All three colleges were organized primarily to educate newly emancipated slaves. Other colleges focused on the technical and scientific needs of the United States. The Morrill Acts of 1862 and 1890 gave states federal lands on which to establish colleges offering programs in agriculture, engineering, and home economics. These institutions were called "land grant" colleges and were dedicated to training people to do the kind of applied research that would advance practical knowledge. Agricultural experimental stations were one example of services developed by these institutions and reflect the thrust toward applied research.

Graduate education made its appearance in the latter part of the nineteenth century. Yale had awarded the first Ph.D. degree in 1861, but it did not offer significant graduate training until the twentieth century. Harvard's first attempts at graduate education were also failures, although in 1869 Eliot of Harvard slowly began to implement an elective system that allowed students to choose at least some of their own courses. Increasingly, however, America had come to believe in social Darwinism, that the world was becoming better as a natural process and that education was a key to gaining fitness and ensuring survival. It was a time that some have characterized as the "Age of Energy," both mechanical and personal.[2]

With the founding of Johns Hopkins in 1876, an institution based on the German model of learning and research, the university era in the United States began. Daniel Coit Gilman, Hopkins' president, changed the face of American education by advocating that its ultimate purpose was to create knowledge that stood on the cutting edge of our understanding. In addition to revising the curriculum, Gilman produced a new breed of professor—one who would be a scholar—and introduced new methods of teaching. Rather than rely on lectures and memorization, students were encouraged to participate in discussion and to engage in independent thought. The seminar approach, highly influenced by laboratory sciences, became the principal method for training graduate students. Faculty no longer thought of themselves only as teachers, but as chemists, historians, and economists. Their audience was composed both of students in the classroom and peers reached through journals, books, and learned society meetings.

The new orientation was accompanied by a cognizance of how poorly prepared students were to meet the increased challenges of higher education. In 1885, with the formation of the New England Association of Colleges and Secondary Schools, whose purpose was to accredit college preparatory schools, the critics' call for more rigorous standards was answered. While standards were emerging, a parallel development found faculty members beginning to bemoan their lack of autonomy in teaching. "Academic freedom," until that time, had signified a student's right to choose elective courses. Faculty members were routinely and arbitrarily dismissed for expressing unpopular views. Organizations composed of faculty from more than a single institution began to form as these scholars recognized coincident interests. In 1915 the American Association of University Professors (AAUP) was established. Originally only an elite group, it gradually came to include all levels of faculty. Among its aims was the promotion of professional rights, especially academic freedom.

The nine early colleges all became research universities, but they also retained a commitment to provide superior educational experiences for undergraduates. Most have remained private and have attracted substantial support from alumni and friends, as well as from federal and state granting agencies.

Not all nineteenth-century colleges developed into universities or research institutions. Many opted to become "colleges" in the twentieth century sense emphasizing baccalaureate rather than advanced degrees. Women's colleges continued to be established. While some offered liberal arts courses, others stressed more practical subjects such as home economics. Women who aspired to graduate schools had to search hard and far for institutions that would accept them. Fellowships were generally available only to men and not every subject was deemed appropriate for women.

Black colleges were founded in greater numbers, many of them state-supported. Often poorly funded and forced to remain segregated, they worked against formidable odds, struggling to survive and to provide their students an adequate education and sufficient training to enable them to function as teachers, preachers, and health workers. Religious denominations accounted for the growth of numerous institutions of higher learning. The United Methodist Church sponsored the development of countless universities and colleges, as did the Roman Catholic Church.

By 1900, there existed special colleges for Baptists and Catholics, for men and women, for whites and blacks, for rich and not-so-rich, for Northerners and Southerners, for small towns and big cities, for adolescents and adults, for engineers and teachers.[3]

Public colleges, as distinct from public universities, commonly had their origins in teacher-training institutions. As the need for educated workers increased, the teaching profession matured and developed greater expectations concerning the qualifications of its members. State legislatures, responding to pressures to supply teachers, created new colleges or authorized the purchase and upgrading of existing ones. Many of these institutions had programs that were less than four years in duration and students were often admitted without having completed four years of high school. Gradually, colleges founded to train teachers broadened their offerings and became alternate paths to higher education. In time, states created systems of public colleges and adopted standards to assure that quality education was being offered. Community colleges emerged as local conduits to four-year institutions. Two-year schools generally taught basic liberal arts courses, ones that formed the nonspecialized core of a bachelor's degree. Other two-year schools began to offer applied terminal degrees in subjects such as firefighting or nursing.

Each state designs its higher education system differently. Implicit in each, however, is a set of shared definitions and assumptions that describe what constitutes the appropriate amount of study, credit and curriculum required to earn a particular degree. These agreements are, in effect, the glue that binds American higher education. The credit system makes possible "stopping out" and transferring. In two year colleges—junior or community—the programs lead to an associate degree. The completion of four years of undergraduate education, either at a college or a university, produces a bachelor of arts or a bachelor of science degree. A baccalaureate degree constitutes the main prerequisite for admission to most graduate and professional programs. One or two years of study beyond the bachelor's generally results in a master's degree. Universities offer doctor of philosophy or professional degrees. By and large, agreements about what constitutes appropriate study for various degrees were made in the early part of the twentieth century with the emergence of professional associations. The formation of a system of institutional accreditation and a parallel system designed to define various specializations and professions were inaugurated through joint efforts of professional associations and state agencies to ensure quality control.

CONTEMPORARY COLLEGES

With the end of World War II and the provision of educational benefits to returning soldiers, the nation's institutions of learning entered an era of significant expansion. The period from 1955 to 1974 witnessed breathtaking growth in higher education. The number of students enrolled in postsecondary institutions burgeoned—rising from 2.5 million in 1955 to 8.8 million in 1974. The percentage of eighteen-year-olds attending college grew from 17.8 in 1955 to 33.5 in 1974. Black student enrollment increased eightfold and the proportion of women students rose from one-third to one-half of all enrollments. Academic institutions, assisted by a variety of federal and state financing sources embarked on ambitious building programs and constructed more dormitories, classrooms, and libraries in the first three decades of the post-World War II period than had been put up in the previous two hundred years. The number of community colleges increased from 400 to 973, and the number of students in these schools grew from 325,000 to 3.4 million.[4]

Distinctions between and among colleges became less apparent. Separation of college students by gender and race, in particular, seemed to be rapidly disappearing. The decision to admit women to previously all-male institutions in the 1960s and 1970s resulted in a decrease of almost two-thirds in the number of women's colleges. Active recruitment of minority students to predominantly white institutions seriously changed these colleges and also had an impact on black colleges, particularly those located in the South.

Many of the early denominational colleges no longer stress their religious underpinnings. They now offer programs quite similar to those available at nondenominational colleges and universities. Other institutions continue to maintain links to the denomination, some tenuous, some firm. Earlham College, for instance, follows the tenets of Quakerism in the way campus decisions are reached. The curriculum at Yeshiva University reflects its ties to Judaism. Colleges sponsored by fundamentalist Protestant sects are likely to adhere very closely to denominational precepts and to base their curricula, social activities, and modes of dress on religious doctrine. At other schools, a particular sectarian ethos may be more ambiguous but remain part of the fabric of the college.

By the 1980s, higher education was experiencing serious problems, including budget shortfalls, reduced numbers of available students, criticism of its curriculum, violation of ethical standards, racism, accusations about inflated emphasis on athletics, and finally, disapproval of the way in which money was handled. These problems continue into the 1990s, with financial concerns and substantially diminished applicant pools among the most serious.

A composite picture of higher education today would reveal 3,632 institutions attended by 14,491,226 students with slightly more than half of the institutions funded by state or local governments and the rest privately funded.[5]

The two-year college is the most prevalent type in America, followed by colleges offering bachelors and/or first professional degrees. In 1995, the *Almanac of Higher Education* identified 2,190 four-year colleges in the United States. About three-quarters of these colleges are privately controlled, many of them church-related, and about one-quarter publicly controlled. Significantly, the public colleges account for more than half the enrollment.[6]

SOCIAL FORCES

Higher education today mirrors the flux of the world in which it is trying to operate. In addition to the remarkable geopolitical events of the past few years, there are other trends that influence the course of academic life. We have become, perforce, a "learning society," in which rapid change requires a lifetime of learning in order to survive. Among the major social forces affecting higher education are:[7]

1. *An aging population.* In 1983, there were more Americans over the age of sixty-five than there were teenagers. The oldest baby boomers, those born between 1946 and 1964, are now in their forties. There has been a commensurate dramatic drop in birthrates. In 1960, there were 23.7 births per thousand population; by 1975, this had fallen to 14.6 per thousand. Although we are in the middle of a new baby boomlet, there will be a dramatic decrease in the number of young adults between the ages of eighteen and twenty-six in the next decade. Demographic projections are now an important variable in planning on most college campuses.

2. *An increase in racial and ethnic diversity.* Birth rates among Blacks and Hispanics remain at higher levels, and immigration is largely from Asia and Latin America. Demographers predict that by 2010 one of every three persons in the United States will be Black, Hispanic or Asian American. A new emphasis on diversity has resulted in multiethnic, multiracial campuses, and institutions are often unprepared for the demands placed on them by new students with such diverse backgrounds.

3. *Shift to a service-oriented global economy.* The economy of the United States is affected by the economy of other countries. The percentage of people involved in farming and manufacturing is decreasing, while the proportion of the population involved in managerial and professional enterprises is increasing. New educational skills are required for those whose jobs have been superannuated by technology and who face the prospect of accepting nonskilled, entry-level service industry jobs. Knowledge of other cultures and languages becomes important for economic as well as cultural reasons. Colleges are expected to contribute to the production and development of skills that provide global opportunities and economic remedies to societal problems.

4. *A proliferation of information.* What was once an industrial society is now an information society. People have easier access to more information than ever before. The amount of information is said to double every seven years. But availability of information does not guarantee better knowledge or ideas. "Information is no more than it has ever been; discrete bundles of facts, sometimes useful, sometimes trivial and never the substance of thought. We must not be tempted to believe that the more information we have, the higher the quality of our thinking and problem-solving will be."[8]

5. *A continuing high illiteracy rate.* Twenty-five million Americans cannot read road signs; 35 million more cannot read well enough to function in society. A learning society presupposes literacy. Without the tools to learn, the information society described above becomes inaccessible.

6. *Changing assumptions about the course of human development.* Most members of contemporary society currently assume that the scientific method is the only valid approach to knowledge. They believe that the universe is a mechanical system composed of elementary material building blocks; that life in society is a competitive struggle for existence; and that material progress for everyone can be achieved through technological and economic growth. Students of society, however, recognize a gradual paradigm shift away from these assumptions. The futurist Alvin Toffler, for instance, contends that there is a fast-spreading recognition that moral, aesthetic, political and environmental degradation will inhibit society no matter how much material or technological progress it has made.

The societal forces listed above have serious consequences for higher education and, of course, ultimately for academic libraries. To fulfill the needs of a "learning society," colleges and universities have been and are being asked to become lifelong institutions, to serve older and part-time students with credit and noncredit offerings, to serve multicultural populations, to serve business, and to serve local communities. The population shifts have resulted in similar changes in student enrollments. The pool of eighteen- to twenty-four-year-olds is declining. In 1983, there were 12.5 million, but the number is expected to be only 11.8 million in 1992. Demographers projected that 49 percent of students in institutions of higher education in 1992 would be twenty-five years old or older; the actual percentage enrolled was 50 percent.[9] Of that number, over 50 percent were women. Among minority groups, young people constitute an even greater percentage of the population. Yet, presently, smaller proportions earn high school degrees.

These population shifts have resulted in changes in the way in which higher education is administered and offered. Three-quarters of older students study part-time, and often only in the evening. Multiculturalism has become a reality on most college campuses and educational leaders see their mission as threefold: to socialize minority students to their institutions and to the majority culture; to socialize white students to the sometimes unfamiliar norms of their minority academic peers; and to socialize both groups to non-Western thinking and values.

Competition among private colleges and universities to fill their classes has been heightened by the changing population, by decreased federal support in aid of students, and by increasing tuition costs at private colleges (a factor that has caused many potential students to opt for public schools). Some fear that competition for students may lead to faddish behavior and "a jumble of programs patched together to pander to every taste."[10]

CURRICULUM

Curriculum reform has swept the nation as critics become increasingly vocal in their condemnation of what is currently being offered to incoming students. Simultaneously there are competing cries for more relevant education, pleas for colleges to return to "the canon" or a new facsimile of it, demands for educators to produce students who can "read and write," and calls for multicultural approaches to learning. Most colleges have recognized the need for remediation and have accepted some responsibility for supplying it. A number of recruiting strategies have surfaced. Cocurricular areas of college life have been stressed in admissions literature. Some colleges have lowered their admissions standards in order to "have a class," that is, to ensure that an adequate number of students matriculate to keep the institution solvent. Other colleges have shifted from a liberal arts orientation toward one with more vocational content. Some have even adopted vocational or occupational majors. Adults generally enroll in courses for job-related reasons, and some colleges try to attract this clientele by altering their curriculum.

A curriculum, according to Phyllis Keller, "is ultimately more than a cluster of courses arranged in an institutionally accepted pattern. It is the statement of a faculty, a college, a generation, as to what they believe to be the character and goals of a college education."[11] Curriculum was hardly a question in the colonial colleges. As described already, it followed the English model and consisted of a prescribed set of courses. When Charles William Eliot became president of Harvard in 1869, he instituted a system of electives whereby students could choose the courses they would take. This innovation, he thought, would allow for individual differences, give students a measure of free choice, offer variety in intellectual opportunities, and facilitate students' gaining depth in one area.

At the time that Eliot introduced electives, students entering Harvard had sufficient preparation to succeed at that institution. Unfortunately, many of the nation's schools that copied Harvard's elective approach recruited students not nearly so well grounded in academic subjects. Gradually, the entrance requirements at Harvard were also lowered as the school endeavored to attract "the brightest boys," those who showed the greatest promise, but who might not have received the classical education provided to students who attended elite preparatory schools. Harvard faculty began to complain that the elective system did not lead to intellectual competency. Teaching staffs in other institutions also lamented the poor preparation of their undergraduates.

Abbott Lawrence Lowell, who acceded to the presidency of Harvard in 1909, replaced Eliot's curriculum with one that required six full-year courses chosen from three fields outside the major. He also instituted a series of concentration requirements. This approach found favor, not only among many of Harvard's faculty, but in the nation's other colleges as well. In the early and mid-twentieth century the concentration-distribution-elective structure became the norm. The intention was to provide a heterogenous student body with common learning and shared intellectual purpose.

Even greater emphasis was put on common knowledge in the general studies curricula attempted at Columbia and Chicago. Columbia retained a few electives, but aimed to provide a comprehensive overview of the main features and significant ideas of Western civilization. Chicago's experiment was more radical. No electives or majors were permitted. The curriculum was wholly prescribed and embodied a series of interdisciplinary courses in humanities, social sciences and natural sciences.

The reformers promoting general education programs insisted that students be made aware of ideas that shaped the society in which they lived and that a common intellectual culture be transmitted.

Harvard's interpretation of general education was that it should have a substantive focus on both heritage, the study of the past to enrich and clarify the meaning of the present, and change, understanding that the scientific method of thought demands data testing before conclusions are reached and that conclusions must be tentative.

Harvard, Columbia, and Chicago built into the general education curricula their belief that there were bodies of essential knowledge— information and ideas—that every student should acquire.

In the late 1970s, Harvard, like most schools in the nation, found itself with sets of courses masquerading as curricula. Demands for "relevancy" in the 1960s and early 1970s had led to a dilution of common materials. Students shared little in the way of a common college experience, and narrow treatments of discrete subjects had replaced an agreed-upon program of learning. After a difficult process of negotiation, Harvard adopted a core curriculum, one that has been widely copied, albeit adapted to the unique needs of individual campuses across the nation. In many ways a return to general education, the new curriculum stresses the major modes of disciplinary thought, rather than specific bodies of literature. Educators have concluded that "it is as important to set a standard of intellectual range for all students as it is to require that they concentrate on a particular subject that engages their interests."[12] They have defined this objective in terms of a set of essential skills and ways of thinking—as starting points for discovering, organizing, and understanding the knowledge they would want or need to acquire later. The products emerging from curriculum reform vary from campus to campus. In elite schools, the research-college model, with its more abstract emphasis on process, exploration, and discovery will prevail. Learning and knowledge will continue to constitute the "profit" of higher education. In schools where students are less well prepared, remediation and basic skills will occupy much of the first- and second-year experience. Vocational training, preparation for a job or an occupation, may monopolize the time of juniors or seniors in undergraduate institutions with a practical interpretation of what constitutes a core.

COLLEGE STUDENTS TODAY

College students today are characterized as poorly prepared, less altruistic, more concerned about self, more anxious about the future. They are less likely to be attending college because of an interest in gaining a general education than for the purpose of acquiring skills that will permit them to be greater wage earners. Today's undergraduates are more middle-of-the-road socially than their predecessors of a decade or two ago, support conservative positions on law and order, and are deeply concerned about the environment.[13] In addition, numbers of students lack basic skills in reading, writing, and computation, resulting in a discontinuity between high school and college. The competing career concerns of faculty have caused them to divide their loyalties between teaching and scholarship, too often favoring the latter at the expense of students.[14] To some, the quality of campus life seems to be deteriorating ,and a sense of common purpose disappearing. Faculty and administrators participate less frequently in college life outside the classroom. In a recent survey of college presidents, alcohol abuse, racial tensions, dilapidated student unions, and the diverse needs of commuter students were identified as major concerns.[15]

KEEPING UP WITH HIGHER EDUCATION

Knowing how to locate information about higher education serves a dual purposes for academic librarians. It permits them, first, to gain and maintain an understanding of their environment, and second, the opportunity to share their particular skills and expertise with their communities. Professionals in any field have an obligation to become intimate with the environment in which they function. Accepting a position in higher education establishes a relationship between an academic librarian and academia that carries with it the duty to understand and participate in that world. Faculty and administrators in colleges regularly make informed judgments about their needs and often base these judgments, at least to some extent, on institutional realities at comparable schools and on trends in higher education.

Higher education is replete with specialized associations established to consider and act on matters of mutual concern.[16] Most private colleges, for instance, join the Association of American Colleges; land grant institutions may choose to identify as members of the National Association of State Universities and Land Grant Colleges. These organizations serve their members through programs of professional development. They help teachers and administrators focus on standards of excellence, and they provide forums for exchanging ideas. They also serve as agencies for lobbying national or state governments about legislation favorable to their members.

Colleges and universities share their concerns in higher education literature as well as through academic organizations. Journals, newspapers, and newsletters inform constituents of current happenings, trends, and ideas. Three publications that address the range of academic issues and that are general in their approach and appeal are the *Chronicle of Higher Education*, *Academe*, and *Change*. The *Chronicle*, as it is commonly called, is an independent newspaper published weekly since 1966. Its columns describe current happenings in institutions of higher learning, report on surveys it and other agencies have undertaken, and publish statistics about enrollments, tuition, state aid, faculty salaries, and student attitudes. The *Chronicle* is also a primary source of information about professional vacancies for faculty, administrators, and librarians. This feature is one that is available on the *Chronicle*'s home page on the Internet along with selected statistics and news summaries.

Academe is published by the American Association of University Professors. It focuses attention on the concerns of faculty and argues for a greater voice for them in the development of sound educational, personnel, and governance policies in all types of colleges and universities. Among its annual reports, the one describing the economic status of the profession is widely used by administrators and faculty to strengthen their relative positions. *Change*, sponsored by the American Council on Education, seeks, as its title implies, to encourage the development of new pedagogical approaches in higher education. While the theme of each issue may vary, the concern for reform and innovation is always present.

Establishing a routing system among librarians for these and similar journals and newspapers encourages members of the library profession to broaden their understanding of higher education, and to make connections between their work and the concerns of faculty and administrators on their campuses. Librarians should also involve themselves in these organizations or consider writing for these journals; communicating with one's peers is part of the process of influencing change in higher education.

In addition to the three general publications, many specialized journals serve the interests of other campus offices—personnel, financial aid, physical plant, and research on higher education, for example. A useful guide to the literature of higher education is Lois Buttlar's *Education: A Guide to Reference and Information Sources.*[17] Beginning in the early 1990s, the Association of College and Research Libraries publication, *College and Research Libraries News* has published a number of bibliographies describing electronic resources related to a variety of disciplines, that are available on the World Wide Web. These are valuable for both reference work and general information about trends in higher education.

Statistical information about higher education is available in a variety of sources. National norms may be interesting. Far more useful to administrators and librarians is information about both comparable and goal or benchmark colleges. Higher education is a status-based hierarchy with a few well-known elite institutions, a larger group with "modest" reputations, and a large group virtually unknown outside their geographic regions. Colleges identify as peers those schools that compete with them for students, share similar goals and missions, are roughly the same size, and are controlled in the same manner (public or private). Colleges identify as model, benchmark or goal institutions those schools that are somewhat more successful in student recruitment and endowment. In most cases, the college administration decides these groupings. Once peer and model institutions have been identified, data about them are used for decision making, long-range planning, and budget allocations.

Among the best sources for ferreting out statistical information about higher education are:

The Chronicle of Higher Education, which reports on all major studies, often summarizing key findings and data; its annual *Almanac of Higher Education* is a compilation of the *Chronicle's* most important data. Parts are available on the *Chronicle* home page on the World Wide Web.

The College Handbook, an annual publication of the College Board, contains up-to-date enrollment figures.

American Universities and Colleges, published by the American Council on Education, gives institutional profiles; the Council's *Fact Book* summaries a broad array of data.

Digest of Educational Statistics, from the U.S. Department of

Education's National Center for Educational Statistics, is another compendium of statistics about all facets of education, including higher education.

A Classification of Institutions of Higher Education, published in 1994 by the Carnegie Foundation for the Advancement of Teaching, reports on groupings of schools with shared characteristics.

SUMMARY

The citizens of the United States from colonial times to the present have evidenced a strong interest in providing education, first to young, elite, white males, and later, to all citizens. Originally established to train preachers and teachers, colleges broadened their goals as industrial society began to require the services of trained employees. When the English method of education with its emphasis on rote learning was replaced by a German model stressing original inquiry at the forefront of knowledge, new importance began to attach to scholarly and research materials. An egalitarian approach to education followed World War II, and returning GI's swelled the ranks of college students. Contemporary higher education is composed of a diverse group of institutions: private, public, secular, nonsecular, two-year, four-year, comprehensive, and research-oriented.

Societal forces today—an aging population, minority groups with limited access to higher education opportunities, and a post-industrial economy in need of highly skilled employees—influence the development of new programs and curricular offerings at colleges.

Compared with previous generations, many college students today are poorly prepared to undertake a rigorous program of study. In addition, they differ from their predecessors of three decades ago in their lack of concern for society and in their growing interest in the environment.

According to Vartan Gregorian, former president of Brown University, four years of undergraduate education will no longer provide a sufficient education. "The three scourges . . . [of education] will be mental gridlock in the form of undigested information, cultural anorexia in the form of self-inflicted ignorance and national amnesia toward our heritage."[18]

NOTES

1. Orvin Lee Shiflett, *Origins of American Academic Librarianship* (Norwood, N.J.: Ablex, 1981), 46.

2. Shiflett, *Origins of American*, 57.

3. Christopher Jencks and David Reisman, *The Academic Revolution* (Chicago: University of Chicago Press, 1977), 2-3.

4. Jerold W. Apps, *Higher Education in a Learning Society* (San Francisco: Jossey Bass, 1988), 33-34.

5. Chronicle of Higher Education, *Almanac of Higher Education 1995* (Chicago: University of Chicago Press, 1995), 3.

6. Chronicle, *Almanac,* 4.

7. Apps, *Higher Education*, 19-27.

8. Apps, *Higher Education*, 24.

9. Apps, *Higher Education*, 29; Chronicle, *Almanac*, 23.

10. Apps, *Higher Education*, 10.

11. Phyllis Keller, *Getting at the Core* (Boston: Harvard University Press, 1982), ix.

12. Keller, *Getting at the Core*, 132.

13. Alexander Astin et al., *The American Freshman: National Norms for 1988* (New York: American Council on Education, 1988), 33-35.

14. Ernest L. Boyer, *College, the Undergraduate Experience in America* (New York: Harper and Row, 1987), 2.

15. *Chronicle of Higher Education, 2* May 1990, 1.

16. "Tip Sheet for Involvement in Non-library Associations, *College and Research Libraries News* 51, (July/August 1990): 632.

17. Lois Buttlar, *Education: A Guide to the Reference and Information Sources* (Littleton, Colo.: Libraries Unlimited, 1989).

18. "Periscope," *Newsweek*, 8 January 1990, n.p.

Chapter 3

GROWTH OF ACADEMIC LIBRARIANSHIP

Beginning with the colonial period, the fortunes of academic libraries have been intimately and inextricably bound to the institutions of which they are a part. Changes in the landscape of higher education found strong echoes in academic library development. Curricula, in particular, have played a crucial role in determining how libraries have been viewed and utilized. However, chance and individual effort are always factors and college libraries in similar institutions have matured and fared differently. The academic library profession evolved slowly, its growth paralleling the increasing importance assigned to books and libraries in the educational process as the nation sought first to educate its elite, white, young men, and later to train all of its people.

EARLY PERIOD

Reading was not an essential occupation of students in colonial colleges. Rather, they learned by means of lectures, memorization, and recitation. Libraries, similarly, had marginal utility in the educational process. But libraries were important to colonial colleges because their holdings contributed to the institution's wealth and prestige. Indeed, the worth of a college was often measured by the value of its library collection. Books were not only considered artifacts of education, but represented tangible evidence that the community's elite supported the institution. Colonial college libraries were almost always the product of gifts. Donors were courted and rewarded; it is no coincidence that Harvard, Brown, and Yale were named for library-conscious benefactors. Without the contribution of private collections, college library holdings would have been negligible.

Books in early college libraries were generally old and often rare. An analysis of John Harvard's donated collection of 250 titles revealed that 65 percent were entered under Latin titles, and that there were eight classes of books: theology (65 percent of the collection), classics, professional (law and medicine), history (a few volumes), philosophy (logic and ethics), poetry (a slight taste), essays, and foreign language (a Spanish-English dictionary).[1]

Scholars who study the early college libraries have concluded that they were designed to keep readers and books apart. Access was a major problem. Consider the situation described in a Harvard report of 1859:

> Just beyond Mr. Sibley's office, there is a spacious and handsome hall, about twenty roomy and comfortable alcoves, all well lighted, ventilated and warmed, furnished with many convenient tables and desks, but showing in many places an advertisement in large type, conspicuously posted up, announcing that "No person is allowed to enter." Without obtaining the special leave from the Librarian, a student may not even seat himself at one of the tables in order to read or write, though most of them are unoccupied nine-tenths of the time. The students' privileges in the body of the building are limited to a permission to walk up and down the long hall in the center, consult the alcove lists and admire the President's busts.[2]

A few randomly selected examples suggest that the problems of access continued for most of the nineteenth century.

In the 1840s Amherst not only kept its books covered with white netting, but opened the library only one hour per week. For fifty years after 1856, the University of Michigan steadfastly refused to loan books to students. In 1878, Columbia University lent books only to those who had the permission of the President. The Library of the University of North Carolina for two decades was located in a bedroom in the President's residence.[3]

With a few notable exceptions, the growth of academic libraries during the period from 1780 to 1830 was a product of luck rather than rational planning. Harvard was one of the few to embark on a policy of systematic collection development, particularly when Joshua Green Cogswell held the position of librarian. The University of Virginia, too, under the tutelage of Thomas Jefferson, tried to create a new kind of utilitarian university library. Regrettably, the effort languished after his death.

The lack of good college libraries produced what came to be known as "society libraries." Student-owned and -operated, their capital derived from self-imposed taxes, these libraries contained books that appealed to the popular reading tastes of undergraduates. Materials which could be used in debates, an important collegiate activity of the period, were also collected and made available. College libraries included scholarly books, major works of reference, rare editions, and esoteric material. Society libraries, on the other hand, contained recent books, modern poetry and essays, biography, and even some fiction. By 1829, society libraries could boast more than half as many volumes as those owned by college libraries. In fact, many college libraries—the ones at Dartmouth, Middlebury, Amherst and Union, for instance—owned fewer books than did their student-controlled counterparts.[4]

Gradually society libraries merged with those of their parent institutions. Far more generous use and acquisition policies had been associated with society libraries than with college libraries. Students accustomed to daily access to the society library expected no less when they gave up their private collections. In addition, they now demanded that the library select materials of interest to them rather than simply purchase or accept blocks of rare books without regard to their potential use.

Real change came to college libraries after the Civil War. While a new, small, denominational college struggling to survive its first ten years might still view books as artifacts and the curriculum as a set of experiences related to memorization and the acceptance of faith, other visions for the role of a college and its library emerged. Teachers and advanced students of biblical exegesis, for instance, began to recognize that mastery of certain scriptural passages might necessitate comparing the translation in several texts. When Johns Hopkins instituted its German-based curriculum emphasizing scientific inquiry, libraries were launched into a new and crucial position on the university campuses.

In college after college acceptance that specialization is appropriate to education, adoption of the elective system for students, availability of more sophisticated courses, all influenced the pressures on college libraries to enlarge. Increasing faculty involvement in and commitment to generating knowledge, and acknowledgment that research was a major function of a university "contributed to the emerging consensus that the library constituted the very 'heart' of any self-respecting academic institution."[5] Scholarly communication brought with it new journals and further fueled the library's role as repository of the latest scientific thought. Some of the surplus wealth developed from commercial and industrial development that had found its way into the treasuries of colleges and universities was channeled into libraries. Institutions established as a result of the Morrill Acts, in particular, benefited from the largesse of this new source of support and their libraries became some of the best in the country. It is fair to say that by the turn of the century the library was believed to be central to the mission of a university. College libraries acceded to that position early in the twentieth century.

EMERGENCE OF A PROFESSION

The office of librarian was one of the first to be differentiated after the presidency in the academic hierarchy of the classical college, but his duties were primarily custodial. He was responsible for carrying the key to the room and seeing to it that it was tightly locked except during the periods of the week when students were permitted to use the books. As the library grew, faculty members continued to serve as librarian, but now they were often joined by a newly graduated, bookish male student to help them with the technical work—ordering and organizing—and to keep the library open for a few additional hours each week. Library work was the province of men until the latter part of the nineteenth century, when a few women were permitted to work as library clerks or as assistant librarians.

Librarianship, including academic librarianship, emerged as a new specialization in the 1870s. The American Library Association was formed in 1876 and led by respected librarians—Melvil Dewey of Columbia and Justin Winsor of Harvard—who called attention to professional concerns and helped to shape an agenda for the field. Establishment of library schools further aided in affirming the identification of librarianship as a profession. Widespread adoption of the decimal classification system formulated by Dewey in 1875 led to better organization, which, in turn, made libraries more serviceable. Now, however, the services of a librarian trained in the mysteries and intricacies of the system were required to classify and catalog materials appropriately.

At the same time that librarianship was emerging as a profession, college faculty, their attention increasingly occupied in instruction and research, were no longer willing to allocate a portion of their time to running the library, which now demanded the services of a full-time person who could be expected to possess technical and specialized knowledge. The older, more elite institutions began to hire graduates of the newly established professional library schools. While persons who might also do some teaching were considered more desirable, the library, rather than the classroom, was their primary work site. In this way, the new librarians, such notables as William Warner Bishop, Andrew Keogh, and Theodore Koch differed from their "scholar librarian" predecesors. Some librarians continued to teach, but most now concentrated on the library.

The new breed of librarian attended, sometimes with missionary zeal, to standardizing the procedures of cataloging, developing efficient systems for handling circulation, and improving the methods of ordering, exchanging, and shelving books. Spurred on by the public library movement, they adopted a philosophy that placed use and service to all over custodianship and protection. They were intent on making more books accessible on open shelves and breaking down the traditional barriers created by viewing the library as a museum, aloof and dignified. Reference services were extended and improved; orientation on the use of the library became widely available; general reading was encouraged through the establishment of browsing rooms, dormitory libraries, weekly book talks; and student library prize awards. In short, library efficiency was improved on most campuses, and a high standard of service was set by the leaders of the new profession. Participation in scholarly activities, however, occurred less frequently.

Unfortunately, the move away from teaching and scholarly pursuits for librarians brought them lower status in the eyes of the academic community. A lessened orientation toward participation in scholarly research, coupled with the now prominent distinction between their administrative responsibilities and classroom teaching resulted in library work being viewed as something of lesser importance that certainly carried diminished educational prestige. The movement of women into the field of librarianship also gave rise among male faculty to skepticism about the profession's academic legitimacy. The proper role of the librarian—manager, scholar, merchant, salesperson—began to capture the attention of librarians in their literature and at their professional meetings. The difficulty of combining all of these roles created an identity problem that still prevails. In short, the modern period of academic librarianship had begun.

TWENTIETH CENTURY

By the start of the twentieth century, academic libraries were growing at a dizzying speed, their collections doubling in size every sixteen years. New service patterns were in evidence—longer hours, better trained staffs, and more efficient methods of operation. Larger collections required greater organization and arrangement, and the adoption of more appropriate classification systems often necessitated recataloging whole collections. Buildings were planned and erected specifically for library purposes, not merely as museums to house artifacts. The library was integrated into the college's academic program. New teaching methods, the seminar approach in particular, generated student research and greater use of library materials. Gradually, faculty began to involve themselves in selection and collection development, motivated by pedagogical reasons as well as by self-interest.

Since their creation in the late nineteenth century, regional accrediting associations had always included libraries as one element to be evaluated on any college campus. But now, standards were being developed to measure the quality of the library, its building, and collections. Prior to 1934, all of the standards were rigid and quantitative in nature, calling for academic libraries, no matter what their individual differences, to contain a certain number of books, periodicals, and pamphlets. Despite the categorical nature of the standards, they were extremely useful to librarians who could utilize them as leverage with administrators to improve inadequate libraries full of inappropriate materials—older books of little interest to faculty or students and housed in cramped quarters. With published standards in hand, librarians were able to argue that poor libraries were an impediment to the educational process and to buttress their contentions by pointing to dictated quantities.

College presidents had always accepted the responsibility for securing outside funding for their libraries. In 1790, the task might have been to obtain a treasured book for the collection from a potential donor; in 1890, the obligation may have been to find a contributor who would help to fund a free-standing library building. In the Depression era of the 1930s, the object was to win foundation support to provide a collection of materials to satisfy the current and next generation of college students.

During the period from 1929 to 1940, several foundations—the most notable of which was the Carnegie Corporation of New York—

instituted studies of various types of college libraries with a view toward making grants to selected institutions. Foundation representatives examined more than a thousand libraries, conferred with college presidents, faculty, and librarians on such problems as the library budget, book and periodical holdings, and staff. According to Louis Round Wilson, these studies exposed the library as a teaching instrument in a way it had never before been seen and revealed to presidents of colleges the adequacy or inadequacy of their libraries as instruments of instruction.[6] Not only did some college libraries profit materially from the Carnegie Corporation following these studies, but as a result of the reports, many others found new prestige accruing to them simply as a result of the attention that had been focused on academic libraries.[7] Another important by-product of the reports was the publication in book form of the findings, including lists of recommended titles and standards for adequate library service, both of which influenced and stimulated institutions that had not received grants to better themselves.

Second in importance only to the Carnegie Corporation grants was the financial assistance given by the General Education Board to library schools for the training of librarians; to various metropolitan areas to establish union catalogs and bibliographical centers; and to individual colleges and universities for book purchases, surveys of libraries, buildings, and equipment, and special library projects. The grants of the General Education Board were most influential in stimulating the development of library facilities as a part of the general college program, and especially in assisting library development in the South.[8] College libraries also benefited from the gifts of the Rockefeller Foundation, which underwrote scholarly publications and bibliographic tools, and contributed to college endowments. The contributions of all three major foundations helped to set a pattern of library giving for smaller foundations.

Another important element in the growth and development of college libraries during this period was the multitude of newly formed "Friends of the Library" organizations. Libraries in the older, better-funded, strong liberal arts institutions still had to depend to some extent upon individual gifts, donations, bequests, and memorials. Some of the finest special collections in the nation's college libraries today had their source in rich private libraries donated or bequeathed to the institution by the owner. Librarians soon realized that even more important than the original gifts were donations and endowments to perpetuate them, and, to this end, substantial energy was spent in cultivating good relationships between donors and the library. To foster a spirit of community, a number of colleges established Friends organizations in the 1930s the chief purpose of which was to preach the gospel of more and better books for the library. Not all were successful, by any means, but those that were generally drew their leadership from alumni and members of the faculty. These Friends organizations served their college libraries both directly and indirectly. They bestowed books or contributed endowments for specific purposes. In addition, they influenced others to donate, placed their librarians in contact with potential donors, and advised them of exceptional bargains in book purchases.

Developments in large public libraries, too, contributed to the strengthening of college libraries during this period. One product of the Depression had been an enlarged educational and social role for public libraries. Their burgeoning clientele borrowed and read increasingly sophisticated material and demanded more intensive reference assistance. College students, used to the services provided by public libraries, expected to find equally well served libraries on their campuses. Large public libraries now offered thousands of books on open shelves, reading and study rooms for subject specialists, exhibition galleries for prints and drawings, discussion groups, film and record loans, and readers' advisory services. They led the way, too, in proposing divisional organization, in introducing audio-visual services, and in the use of labor-saving devices.

Publishing expanded, and unprecedented numbers of books were rolling off the presses. Curriculum reform, as described in chapter 2, led to methods of teaching that could no longer be satisfied by single textbooks. At first the major impact on the library was constant pressure to duplicate required materials. Later, honors and general reading courses, tutorial plans, and other curricular innovations contributed to a different kind of library use and resulted in a demand for new types of material. These two library developments—the substitution of assigned library readings in place of textbooks and the introduction of independent study and research—introduced major changes in the way in which college libraries provided service. The adoption of the reserve reading program brought out of the stacks many books that had previously merely gathered dust. The consequences for libraries of honors theses and student research was somewhat less noticeable because at first, faculty rarely exploited the library's role in connection with these programs. Nevertheless, the broad and deep use which resulted from some student research encouraged numbers of faculty and librarians to push for more active participation by the library in the general scheme of college education.

The Depression of the late 1920s and 1930s had seriously effected college and university libraries, just, it seemed, as they were coming into their own. For some libraries, this meant delaying their building programs. Budgets and staffs were slashed. Some help had come in the form of federal aid obtained through the Works Project Administration (WPA), which provided assistance in binding, cataloging, indexing, and building repairs in some publicly funded institutions. Most libraries fell behind in collection development, reference services, and new construction. Ironically, the Depression produced a number of salutary effects, according to Michael Harris, the most important of which was that it caused librarians to "pause and reflect on their nature and purpose in the general education scene"[9] and stimulated attempts to find alternate ways of extending service despite their diminished budgets. Overcrowding, for instance, which could not be met with new buildings, generated experimentation with new forms of storage including a variety of microforms. The lack of sufficient materials gave rise to interlibrary loan, and cooperative acquisitions programs, which, while limited, achieved some measure of success.

POST-WORLD WAR II LIBRARIES

When World War II ended, the majority of colleges and their libraries were in dire financial straits. Fortuitously, demands by veterans for higher education, coupled with federal legislation (commonly known as the GI Bill) to fund it, not only solved the capital problem, but fueled an era of rapid expansion of services, faculties and, indeed, colleges themselves. Academic libraries shared in the boom, augmenting and strengthening their collections and services. Despite the use of new storage techniques and the widespread transfer of newspapers to microfilm, library stacks were once again at capacity. Collections were now estimated to double every ten years. By the 1950s, most colleges had erected totally new structures or put additions on existing ones.

College librarians were called upon to supply not only substantial quantities of traditional library materials, but also to make available a variety of the newer instructional aids to meet the needs of new types of students who were streaming into all kinds of institutions of higher education. In some instances, particularly at the junior college level, the library was no longer thought of as the place that housed books and journals, but rather as an instructional materials center with responsibility for a whole range of books and mechanical teaching aids. The role of libraries as active participants in the educational process itself was enhanced by these new responsibilities. More and better library services also required enlarged staffs. Librarians were in short supply, their ranks decimated by the Depression and World War II. It was necessary to recruit thousands of new workers to the field.

The impetus to increase service further accelerated with the launching of Sputnik, the first Russian space vehicle, in 1957. The Higher Education Acts (HEA) of 1963 and 1965 provided funds for college library resources, for training librarians, and for research in library science. The five years of federal aid for academic library buildings from 1967 through 1971 have been characterized as "the greatest flowering of academic library experience this county has ever known."[10] HEA guidelines were specific about the importance of equalizing educational opportunities for disadvantaged students, particularly in urban areas. A number of previously substandard institutions were able to reach parity as a result of HEA funds. Federal grants were also available for purposes of experimentation and research in academic librarianship. A revision of the Federal Depository Law made it possible for a great many smaller academic libraries to choose by series and groups of publications what they needed from the vast output of U.S. government publications and to become selective depositories under this act. Regional depositories were created, thereby reducing the pressure on libraries to collect everything and allowing them to become more flexible about the maintenance of documents collections in perpetuity. Today, the well-established federal role stresses research, development of new technologies, and recruitment.[11]

Foundation support continued as well. Ford, U.S. Steel, and other corporate foundations made grants to building, book, and special bibliographical projects. In 1956, the Ford Foundation established the Council on Library Resources (CLR) with the purpose of assisting in "the solution of problems of libraries generally, but more especially of the problems of research libraries by conducting or supporting research, demonstrating new techniques and methods, and disseminating the results."[12] The CLR made important grants for the development of technology; for studies in academic library management; for fellowship programs that would help mid-career librarians widen their experience; for network-based systems; and for book-preservation research, improvement of library equipment, and numerous Library of Congress projects. Later, the National Endowment for the Humanities (NEH) encouraged libraries to apply for challenge grant funds. Successful college library applicants built buildings, developed and preserved special collections, and organized some new services with monies from these sources.

Many college libraries never profited from the immediate post-war boom or foundation support and continued to work under inadequate conditions with insufficient resources. Black colleges, small church-supported institutions—particularly those in the South and in rural areas—had meager collections and small staffs. As they had in the past, standards became helpful to these under-funded, unequipped libraries. Accrediting associations' clout increased, and they began to withhold accreditation. In 1934, the North Central Association had adopted the principle of measuring a college in terms of its program, rather than by absolute and unwavering quantitative measures. The library segment, assigned to Douglas Waples of the University of Chicago Library School, had produced basic qualitative and quantitative criteria for measuring the relative educational value of college libraries. These more realistic standards were then used by libraries to point out the deficiencies of their buildings, collections, staffs, and equipment.

Since they were first adopted, standards have undergone frequent revisions. Today's standards represent the aggregate experience of the profession, rather than the wisdom or experience of individual experts.[13] The most recent standards for college libraries were adopted by the Association of College & Research Libraries in 1995. A copy of them appears in the appendix of this book.

In the recession period of the 1970s, college libraries began to suffer reductions in federal and grant support. In the 1980s, the reduction often came from the institution's inability to meet the cost of library material's inflation fully. Library materials (especially periodicals) and library employees were the subject of retrenchment plans. New librarians, just recently in short supply, suddenly found themselves without the prospect of employment. College libraries, now large and complex, and without sufficient staff to take care of the enormous increase in routine work, looked eagerly for ways to increase productivity. Technology and increased cooperation in the face of the heavy demand and the "information explosion" promised to provide a partial answer and, indeed, have resulted in major changes in the way college libraries operate in the 1990s. Emphasis has shifted to "access" from "acquisition," and networking and automation have become part of every librarian's vocabulary. In the 1960s, OCLC, formerly the Ohio College Library Center, now the Online Cooperative Library Center, was established to provide a computerized cooperative cataloging and union catalog service to a small group of regional libraries. By the 1970s it had greatly expanded its program and spawned similar bibliographic networks throughout the country. Today, it contains more than 21 million records and counts among its members eleven thousand libraries. Other cooperative projects included the Research Libraries Network (RLIN) designed to serve research libraries with shared cataloging, interlibrary loan, serials control, and acquisitions assistance. New materials delivery services, both electronic and manual, made their appearance. On-line databases became widely available, as did off-line electronic data bases in CD-ROM format. Colleges began to boast of being "wired campuses," and library buildings were altered to make them "smart," that is, amenable to sophisticated technology. In addition, new methods of library instruction were developed as librarians sought to increase their participation in the teaching mission of the institution.

By the 1990s, the college library had achieved a position of strength in the educational program and commanded greater respect than ever before from the faculty. The cumulative effect of sustained individual library efforts, the example of successful integration of the library into the teaching program in the smaller progressive colleges, and the support of accrediting associations and foundations all helped to give credence to the significance of the college library's role in facilitating teaching and learning.

What lies ahead? How can college libraries maintain and improve the variety of services they now offer? Surely, the answer lies in cooperation between college administrators, faculty and librarians about the role, function, and operation of the library. The library can only improve if administrators, whose task it is to ensure continued financial support, and faculty, who bear primary responsibility for its use, see the need to strengthen the library. It is incumbent on librarians to continue to lead their constituents through the labyrinth of information and to reaffirm the principle that knowledge, not data, is the goal of education. In addition, they must continue to maintain their stewardship over the materials of cultural heritage and scholarly research so that future generations may have also access to their contents.

PROFESSIONAL INVOLVEMENT

Librarians should involve themselves in enterprises beyond the immediate boundaries of their particular jobs, participate in the work of professional associations, and, when appropriate, contribute to the literature of the field. Most librarians, like workers in other professions, devote only a fraction of their energy to diagnosis, planning, innovation, deliberate change, and growth. Day-to-day considerations demand that the major proportion of available effort be spent in carrying out routine, goal-directed operations and maintaining existing relationships within the system. There is always another library instruction course that can be offered, or a new library handbook to be tackled. Participation in professional life, however, not only expands the individual, but insures the well-being of the profession.

Professional associations can help to bind together the community and mediate relationships between practitioners and the profession, as well as between practitioners and the outside world. They speak for the profession and provide avenues of communication. In more tangible terms, professional associations try to safeguard the welfare of their members, improve working conditions, press for advancement opportunities, and work toward legally enforced standards of professional competence.[14] In addition, they can influence the quality of personnel that the profession recruits.

The American Library Association (ALA) is an umbrella organization for librarians whose purpose is to advance the goals of libraries and librarians. Membership is voluntary. Within ALA, the largest division, the Association of College and Research Libraries (ACRL), is composed mostly of librarians serving in institutions of higher education. Formed in 1889, ACRL has a roster of more than ten thousand members. In addition to sponsoring meetings where matters of interest to librarianship and libraries are discussed, ACRL runs regional training sessions and workshops, and has an extensive publishing program. Among its important publications are the book review journal, *Choice*, and the monthly publication, *College and Research Libraries*, a peer-reviewed journal that publishes research findings as well as essays on topics important to academic librarians. ACRL also publishes *College & Research Library News*, a monthly newsletter that reports on association matters and activities or projects undertaken by academic libraries. Other functions of ACRL are to encourage research and publication; to develop and publish standards, guidelines, and manuals on various aspects of college libraries; to conduct training sessions for librarians; and to work with ALA's legislative office and other organizations devoted to higher education to lobby for legislation that will benefit academic libraries.

The other publication of general interest to college and university librarians is the *Journal of Academic Librarianship*, which also bases its acceptance of articles on peer review and includes reports of research as well as symposia on controversial academic library questions. College libraries are also the subject of a Haworth Press biannual journal begun in 1994, *College and Undergraduate Libraries*.

Librarians involved in a particular phase or specialization of academic librarianship normally ally themselves with others who perform similar functions, joining, for instance, the Reference & User Services Association, the Library Administration and Management Association, the Library and Information Technology Association, and the Association for Library Collections and Technical Services. All of the major components of ALA have their own publications. In addition, there are electronic list serves accessible through the World Wide Web such as COLLIB, a discussion list moderated by Larry Oberg at Willamette University.

The majority of academic librarians earn that designation by virtue of having completed a master's degree in librarianship in an ALA-accredited library program. Since its inception at Columbia University in 1887, library education has been the subject of endless debate about whether it is appropriately designated as professional education or graduate (scholarly) education. The matter is complex, and most institutions waffle, providing both a smattering of theoretical background and sufficient library skills to make graduates feel somewhat competent. In recent years, there has been increased emphasis on understanding research and research methods, partially in response to academic librarians' calls for faculty status. This view of the academic librarian as researcher/practitioner is controversial and has not been fully embraced. Those who advocate full faculty status for academic librarians find it consistent with the role they envision for librarians. Others, who distinguish between faculty as researchers and librarians as practitioners, feel that the emphasis on research and writing places librarians, with work schedules already too full and discretionary time essentially nonexistent, in an untenable positon.

Even for those who make the distinction between practice and research, professional ethics oblige librarians to keep current in the field through independent and formal continuing education, and to add their individual contributions to the collective power of the professional community.

In the nineteenth and early twentieth centuries, academic librarians serving as directors of academic libraries generally had earned a doctorate in one of the classical disciplines. Although the MLS degree is considered a terminal degree, there is a trend toward academic librarians having second master's degrees and, to a lesser extent, doctor of philosophy degrees. While many college librarians hold second master's degrees and a substantial number of directors have doctorates in librarianship, management, or education, a subject doctorate is much less common among contemporary library managers.[15] The question of whether to earn a second master's degree (in addition to the library degree) in a subject discipline or in an information-related specialty is often posed and receives no uniform response. Both courses have value. Study beyond the bachelor's degree in a physical or natural science certainly leads to increased marketability, as does advanced study in any other area with fewer than the desired number of qualified candidates for available positions.

Academic librarians are currently accorded higher status in the profession than librarians from public and school libraries.[16] This may be attributable to the greater number of academic librarians with advanced degrees, a higher percentage of male librarians in academic librarianship, or simply status by association with the prestige of an academic institution. Until recently there has been a tendency in the profession to assume that bigger is better—perhaps richer, more complex—and to hold directors of university libraries in higher esteem than those who head libraries in colleges. As a result, a tilt toward the very large institutions is apparent in the assistance offered to the profession by federal agencies and foundations, in unequal access to grant funds, and in the preparation of graduates by library schools. These attitudes have undergone a gradual change, although to some extent they still prevail. Librarians at smaller academic institutions, however, can claim special rewards. They have unparalleled opportunities to interact with students in library and nonlibrary venues, to build excellent, carefully selected collections, to influence programs of instruction, and, often, a chance to participate in the life of the entire community.

SUMMARY

The history of academic librarianship reflects the history of higher education, but also demonstrates how librarians carved out their own identities as conservators and creative promoters of the records of culture by developing methods to acquire, organize, and disseminate information. The efforts of previous generations of academic librarians to ensure professionalism by forming associations, establishing library schools and devising standards are validated by the several thousand people who call themselves academic librarians and who work together to define and deliver quality services to colleges.

Academic libraries profited from the new importance attributed to scholarship in the late nineteenth century when they were promoted from mere appendage to "heart of the institution." By the 1990s, college libraries had achieved a position of strength in the educational program. Libraries will continue to command respect if they lead their constituents through the labyrinth of information and maintain their guardianship over the materials of cultural heritage and scholarly research so that future generations may also have access to their contents.

NOTES

1. Louis Shores, *Origins of the American College Library 1630-1800* (Nashville, Tenn.: George Peabody College, 1934), 57.

2. Orvin Lee Shiflett, *Origins of American Academic Librarianship* (Norwood, N.J.: Ablex, 1981), 33.

3. David Kaser, "Collection Building in American Universities," in *University Library History*, ed. James Thompson (New York: K.G. Saur, 1980), 39-40.

4. Kaser, "Collection Building," 38.

5. Michael Harris, *History of Libraries in the Western World* (Metuchen, N.J.: Scarecrow Press, 1984), 233.

6. Louis R. Wilson, "The Use of the Library in Instruction," in *Proceedings of the Institute for Administrative Offices of Higher Education, 1941*, ed. John D. Russell (Chicago: University of Chicago Press, 1942), 115-27.

7. Thomas R. Barcus, *Carnegie Corporation & College Libraries 1938-1943* (New York: Carnegie Corporation of New York, 1943).

8. ALA College and University Postwar Planning Committee, *College and University Libraries and Librarianship* (Chicago: American Library Association, 1946), 69-72.

9. Harris, *History of Libraries*, 237.

10. Guy R. Lyle, *The Administration of the College Library*, 4th ed. (New York: H. W. Wilson, 1974), 7.

11. ACRL Task Force on WHCLIS, "Position Paper on Academic Libraries," *College and Research Libraries News* 51 (September 1990): 713-15.

12. Lyle, *Administration*, 7.

13. David Kaser, "Standards for College Libraries," *Library Trends 31* (Summer 1982): 9.

14. Anthony Abbott, *System of Professions* (Chicago: University of Chicago Press, 1988), 35.

15. Jean-Pierre V.W. Herubel, "The Ph.D. Librarian: A Personal Perspective," *College and Research Libraries News* 51 (July/august 1990): 626-28.

16. Pauline Wilson, *Stereotype and Status: Librarians in the United States* (Westport, Conn.: Greenwood Press, 1982).

Chapter 4

CAMPUS CONTEXT

All colleges are products of the same general components. The generic college has students, a faculty, an administration, trustees, alumni, a physical plant, history, traditions, and a library, although no two colleges combine components in equal proportions. The particular mixture, however, is what determines the institution's character and renders it unique. The elements themselves, examined separately, reveal information essential to all participants in campus life who aspire to understand the campus culture and the library's place within it, including, of course, the library director and staff. The library professional contemplating employment with a college who makes a decision based solely on the library, without considering its environment as well, is indeed shortsighted.

CAMPUS INVENTORY

A prospective employee undertaking an inventory of a college would require answers to a variety of questions about the institution. The ones raised here represent a broad range of college life.[1] What the answers may imply about a college are often subject to varying interpretation. For instance, a low faculty turnover rate can mean a stagnant environment or one that provides a highly satisfying milieu for scholar-teachers. Other data would be required before even a tentative conclusion could be reached about the relationship between faculty turnover rates and faculty productivity and morale.

Most of the items below have importance in a very direct way for the library. Using information generated by responses to the questions, the library's constituents can be described and their needs identified. The book collection and the nature of the bibliographic instruction program, for example, should reflect the educational background, achievement, and goals of both students and faculty. The library's funding will be, to a large extent, a product of the college's financial condition and approach to learning and teaching.

Data required to provide adequate responses to most of the questions can be found in published sources, including the guides to four-year colleges used by high school seniors. Documents located in the campus institutional research office offer more details. Not all questions are of equal importance, especially to a new employee, but those that are more significant have been marked with an asterisk. Librarians seeking directorships probably require at least general answers to most of the matters raised. A careful mix of reading on and between the lines of published documents, interviews, and observations will reveal the necessary information. The college catalog, often considered a contract between students and the institution, is a rich source of material about many of the inventory items.

Virtually all of the questions produce measurable data, which can be compared with numbers produced by like institutions. However, care must be taken to ensure that the figures are genuinely comparable and based on similar inputs. Statistics of this kind are relatively easy to manipulate, and, unfortunately, many institutions knowingly or inadvertently engage in deceptions based on incomplete or misleading data. For instance, colleges wishing to underplay a student attrition rate may present the numbers in terms of the previous year's graduates compared with the number of the current entering class and devise a percentage from that. However, no indication is given of what constitutes that graduating class—for instance, how many have taken six or seven years to complete their studies, or whether incoming class sizes are comparable.

Two difficulties become apparent while attempting to develop items for an inventory. The first is determining when to stop asking questions, and the second is deciding whether the really important questions have been included. A twelve-category scheme has been devised to accommodate the inventory questions. The first category places the college in its proximate physical environment. The second category considers the physical plant. The third covers those factors that apply to the institution as a whole. The next five categories include questions concerning groups in the college community—faculty, students, administration, alumni and trustees.[2] The next two segments relate to the curriculum and campus life. The next category deals with services that the institution provides, and the final segment poses four questions about the library.

SITING

Where a college is located can, to some extent, predict and explain who attends that institution. It can also help to determine the kind of campus social life that exists as well as whether a wide-ranging public events program is necessary or desirable. Geographically isolated colleges that attract a diverse nonlocal student body may have a greater need to build community among campus constituents, to offer a more fully developed social life, and to attach great importance to importing outside speakers and cultural entertainment. The reverse may be true in each instance for urban colleges. Questions about the location of a college might include:

1. Where is the college located in terms of urban, suburban, or rural environment? How big is the community?
2. Is it a residential or a commuter college?*
3. Where is the college located within that environment? Residential area? Industrial area? Depressed area?
4. Is there transportation in and out of the campus and the community?
5. What is the community's socio-economic status?
6. What are the community's resources?
7. How near is the college to other academic institutions?
8. What is the town-gown relationship?
9. What is the economy of the area and what is the economic forecast of the region for the next decade?
10. Where is the library located on the campus?*

PHYSICAL PLANT

Good housing, academic buildings and equipment facilitate a college's ability to provide a quality education. For instance, the proportion of students housed on campus, off campus, and in fraternities may reflect attitudes toward social interaction among students. Some of the important questions related to this category are:

1. How many buildings of each kind (classrooms, offices, dormitories, etc.) are there, and what are their age and condition?
2. Are there sufficient buildings to meet campus needs? For

instance, are there adequate numbers of classrooms, etc.? How many students live on campus? in Fraternities? Off campus?

3. Is there a building program in force?
4. What new buildings are most needed or desired?
5. What is the nature of the campus security program?
6. What is the condition of the grounds and outdoor facilities?
7. What are the recreational facilities?
8. What percentage of the campus is accessible to the handicapped?
9. What is the age, condition, and projected capacity of the library?*
10. Is there a campus-based computer network?*

ETHOS

Under this rubric are contained questions that relate to the institution as a whole, that is, its traditions, history, goals, plans, funding, affiliations, and other college-wide considerations. Recently, some colleges have identified themselves as "research colleges," while others consider themselves "liberal arts colleges." Other colleges are oriented toward vocational or occupational training. The first group contends that the best education is produced through research—both faculty and student. The second maintains that the educated student is a product of the process by which they are introduced to the important works of human thought and are trained to deal with them critically. Those in the third group feel that they must be instrumental in producing marketable students.

1. Is the institution public or private?
2. What is its history? How old is it? Are there famous graduates? What have been the trends over time? What are its unique traditions?
3. What are its affiliations? Is it associated with a religious denomination? If so, does the affiliation translate into policy? What are its professional memberships?
4. Is it accredited? Regionally? In academic disciplines?
5. Does it have clearly stated objectives and goals?
6. Does it have a long-range plan that mirrors these objectives?
7. What is its endowment? What is its wealth relative to comparable institutions?
8. What is its budget? What values are implicit in how the budget

is apportioned? Does the budget indicate a stable and healthy economic situation?

9. What is its tuition? What percentage of its budget is represented by tuition?
10. How successful is it in attracting foundation support?
11. Which institutions does it consider either comparable and/or model colleges?*
12. What are some recent changes that faculty, students, and administrators consider significant?

FACULTY

The nature of the faculty, its role, recruitment, evaluation and treatment are crucial factors in determining the well-being of an institution. Education at the traditional liberal arts college was controlled by its faculty. All policy decisions concerning students and curriculum, even peripheral ones, were made by them. In recent years, many campuses have experienced a large growth in the administrative sectors of their institutions, and a new definition and separation of responsibilities may lead to contention and division between faculty and administrators. Among the questions that might be posed under this heading are:

1. How many faculty are there? What is the student-faculty ratio? Has there been growth or shrinkage in the size of the faculty?
2. What is the gender, race, and nationality of the faculty? What is the male-female ratio? Are there minority group members?
3. How many Ph.D.'s are on the faculty? Where were their degrees earned? What were the dissertation topics?
4. Which undergraduate institutions did faculty attend?
5. How old is the faculty? How many are close to retirement? How many are at the beginning of their academic careers?
6. How long have they been at the college?
7. What is the turnover rate among faculty? Does this vary by department? To what institutions are faculty going when they leave?
8. What is the tenure experience? How many are tenured? How many are eligible for tenure ? What percentage is granted tenure?
9. What is the distribution of faculty within ranks?
10. What is the distribution of faculty by department?

11. What is the publishing history and behavior of the faculty?
12. Is there institutional support for research? For other forms of faculty growth and development?
13. What is the sabbatical policy?
14. How successful are faculty in gaining outside funding for their research?
15. What are average faculty salaries by rank and what does the benefits package contain?
16. Are the faculty represented by unions?
17. What is the extent of participation in the American Association of University Professors (AAUP)?
18. How are new faculty recruited?
19. What is the distribution of teaching loads within the college?
20. What is the workload, including academic advising and community service?
21. How are faculty evaluated? Are selection, promotion, and tenure considerations clear and uniformly applied?
22. What criteria weigh most heavily in evaluation of faculty?*
23. Is there a commitment to academic freedom?
24. Is there a policy on parental leave?
25. Is salary information public? Are there salary ranges?
26. Are librarians considered faculty? Do they teach or serve as advisors to students?*

STUDENTS

A college's ability to attract and retain a student body is vital to its existence. The nature of the student body predicts, to some extent, the kinds of teaching the faculty will offer, the kinds of programs that will be devised for students, and the experiences students may encounter during their college careers. The questions posed below represent an abbreviated list, those we consider most important. A substantially more developed list of items that relate to college students, specifically to incoming students, as well as the normative answers can be found in *The American Freshman: National Norms,* issued annually by the Cooperative Institutional Research Program of the American Council on Education, the so-called Astin Reports.[3] Participating colleges contribute data from which national norms are established. The information is used by colleges to compare themselves nationally with like institutions and to track in-house changes over time.

1. How many students are there? What are the student-faculty and student-advisor ratios?
2. Where are the students from geographically? What is the urban-rural breakdown? How many international students are there?
3. What is the gender and racial breakdown? How willing is the college to invest in groups traditionally barred from higher education?
4. From what socioeconomic groups does the college draw? What, for instance, are the occupations and earnings of their parents? What is the family's educational background?
5. Where did students receive their secondary education? What is the breakdown among private vs. public or parochial high schools?
6. What are their religions and religious orientations?
7. What are their SAT or ACT scores? (This figure should not be an average, but the full range for both verbal and quantitative results.)*
8. What rank did students hold in their high school classes?
9. What percentage of students who apply are accepted? What percentage of those accepted are enrolled?
10. What is the degree of institutional commitment to support students who require financial aid? Is admission "need blind"?
11. How many students require remediation?
12. What is the attrition-retention rate and the cohort survival rate?
13. What percentage of the student body is part-time? How many older students are there?
14. What percentage of students do honors work?*
15. What issues concern students as revealed in the student newspaper or in senior exit surveys?
16. What percentage of students work part-time while attending school? How many work on campus?

ADMINISTRATION

On many college campuses there are strong divisions between the administration and the faculty. Students also find themselves in conflict with administrators. Without farsighted administrators whose vision encompasses the entire institution, its mission, and role, the campus cannot function optimally. Among the questions that might be posed about the administration are:

1. What is the size of the administration? How big is it in relation to the faculty and the student body?
2. What are the main administrative offices? How do the offices relate to one another?
3. What is the gender and racial breakdown of the administsrative staff?
4. What is the president's academic and professional background?
5. What kinds of academic and professional backgrounds do other key administrators have, including the library director? How have they been educated?
6. How are they recruited? Is there promotion from within?
7. What are the salary ranges? How do they compare with faculty compensation?
8. What is the turnover rate?
9. What is the management style of the college at present?
10. What is the faculty and student role in governance?*

ALUMNI

The successful undergraduate institution commands great loyalty from those who have completed its program. Alumni may play an important role in the life of the institution financially and in recruitment, as well as in other ways. Answers to the following questions would help to indicate the degree of involvement of alumni in the college:

1. How many alumni are there? Of those, how many can be considered active and how many inactive?
2. What does the college know about them?
3. What percentage have higher degrees?
4. What are their current occupations?
5. How many contribute to the annual fund or to special funds?
6. How many return to the campus or attend local alumni meetings?

TRUSTEES

The governing board of a college is expected to oversee the institution and to hold it accountable. The major duties of the board are to appoint a chief executive officer, develop policies, and make sure the institution is fiscally sound. A more detailed description of the board's responsibilities appears in chapter 5, in which governance is explained. The questions posed here are directed more toward board membership than they are toward legal responsibility.

1. How many board members are there?
2. What are their backgrounds, ages, and current occupations?
3. How many are alumni?
4. How long have they served on the board? What is the turnover?
5. Does the board have a relationship with the National Association of Governing Boards?
6. To what extent do (and must) board members contribute financially to the college?
7. What, if any, interaction is there between board members and faculty and/or students?

CURRICULUM AND ACADEMIC PROGRAMS

Curriculum reform is a fact of life at most American four- year colleges today. Unhappiness with the education of students, both at the secondary and college level, has led to major curriculum overhaul, and reinstatement in one form or another of distributional requirements that include the skills that faculty and administrators wish students to possess at graduation. In many institutions the lack of consensus about what the new curriculum should look like has led to a convoluted approach to requirements—one from group A and two from group B and three from group C—which dissatisfies major segments of the faculty and confuses students. Therefore, it is somewhat difficult therefore, to pose the appropriate curriculum questions. Those that follow are sufficiently general to be germane to most colleges today. Consideration of various pedagogical approaches to education, and their impact on the library, is saved for later chapters.

1. Is there a relationship between the stated goals of the curriculum and the courses offered?
2. When was the curriculum last evaluated and what major changes resulted from the evaluation?
3. How do departments compare with each other in size of faculty, number of students served and class size?
4. What are the popular majors?
5. How many new courses are introduced each year?
6. Have there been new majors and minors adopted recently?

7. What are the requirements for graduation?
8. Are there summer classes?
9. Are there special programs, such as study abroad, independent projects, senior theses, internships, interdisciplinary studies?
10. How do librarians learn about new curricular efforts?

CAMPUS LIFE

Campus life is lived both in and out of the classroom. A variety of activities and experiences are offered on most college campuses to enrich and enliven the institution. In this category appear such important educational and extracurricular programs as speakers, public performances, and athletic participation. Among the questions that might be asked are:

1. How extensive are the public events and speaker-visitor programs? How often are students exposed to well-known professionals in all walks of life?
2. To what extent are students offered the opportunity to participate in cultural events, such as plays, musical performances, and art shows? What percentage participate?
3. What writing and broadcasting outlets are available to students?
4. How important are intercollegiate sports? How many students participate? Is there an even-handed approach to men's and women's athletics?
5. Is there a well-developed intramural program? How many students participate?
6. Is there a student government? How many students participate? What is its role in the extra-curricular life of the campus? Does it have financial resources?
7. Are there fraternities and sororities? What is their role on the campus? What percentage of students participate?
8. What relationships do campus organizations have with external ones?
9. What opportunities exist for interaction between faculty and students outside the classroom?
10. Are there service opportunities for students in the geographic community in which the college is housed?

SERVICES

Most colleges provide a variety of services for the campus. Some of these are directed solely or mainly at students. Others can be utilized by the college community as a whole. Technology and a new understanding of the importance of psychological and career services have resulted in a mushrooming of personnel whose job it is to offer these services. Among the questions to ask here are:

1. Does the college have a career-development or placement office? Whom does it serve?
2. Is there a psychological counseling office? Is it available only for students? Does it include drug and alcohol counseling as well?
3. Are there health services? Who may use them?
4. How accessible are computers and computer training? For whom?
5. Is there daycare for children of employees and for children of students?
6. How developed is the student advising program?
7. What is contained in the orientation programs for students, for faculty, and for administrative employees?
8. Does the bookstore carry trade books as well as textbooks and convenience items?
9. Are there any support groups or services available to particular audiences, such as women, minorities, homosexuals, students needing tutoring, or those from other countries?

LIBRARY

A potential college library employee would have scores of questions concerning the library. Other new college employees, faculty and administrators, should be interested in some aspects of the library. Some questions have been posed about the library under appropriate headings. However, a few additional matters seem essential to consider:

1. What are the strong collections of the library?
2. What are the library's evident needs?
3. What is the nature of the library instruction program?
4. How involved are librarians on campus? Do they participate

in the institution's governance, curriculum decisions, extra-curricular affairs and social life?
5. What is the pattern of staff turnover and promotion in the library?
6. What are the recurring compliments/complaints received by the library staff?

One could gather the information provided by the answers to the questions above, analyze it, and still not have a real grasp of a particular college. Obviously, the institution is more than the sum of all of these parts. Another series of considerations whose answers are less tangible, and more subjective, is described in the following chapter, where attention is turned to governance and politics.

A substantial group of extremely important questions regarding "outcomes" of the college experience are left both unasked and unanswered, yet should not be ignored. For instance, the extent to which the institution has enabled students to make moral choices is surely among the important questions one could pose about a college. The degree to which students are able to gather and evaluate information is another mark of the success or failure of an institution. The librarian has an important role to play in developing these skills, one which will be discussed in later chapters as the role of the library in the educational process is explored.

SUMMARY

Learning about a college is a complex process, one that can sometimes engage the energies of an intelligent seeker for a lifetime. Snapshot views resulting from inventories taken in a moment of time serve as indicators of the strengths or weaknesses of a school. Data gathered from this kind of "institutional scanning" should be compared with information about similar schools and balanced against general demographic and economic indicators. While all colleges have similar components—faculty, students, administrators, alumni, trustees, curricula, physical plants, and, of course, libraries—their individuality lies in how they have traditionally provided for these elements and how these elements are meshed.

NOTES

1. Middle States Association of Colleges and Schools, Commission on

Higher Education, *Characteristics of Excellence in Higher Education* (Philadelphia: Middle States Association, 1994). Regional accreditation standards are often organized around goals and major program areas, and can be used to examine a campus. Ernest Boyer, *College: The Undergraduate Experience in America* (New York: Harper & Row, 1987) is a recent report of the Carnegie Foundation for the Advancement of Teaching that serves as an overview of campus life.

2. The assumption here is that the campus is a community composed of administrators, faculty, students, alumni, and trustees, all playing their roles in the fulfillment of a goal—to create an educational institution. Some models of colleges are student-centered, presupposing that the college exists only to educate students, with all energy directed to that purpose. Others are faculty-centered—driven by the concept that faculty are the core of the institution. Yet others are organized around the notion of an administrative hierarchy. These approaches, while not necessarily mutually exclusive, each provide a somewhat different orientation toward college work and life.

3. Alexander Astin et al., *The American Freshman: National Norms for Fall 1993* (New York: American Council on Education; Los Angeles: University of California at Los Angeles Higher Education Research Institute, 1994). Commonly called the Astin Report.

Chapter 5

LEGAL STATUS, GOVERNANCE, AND POLITICS

Legal status refers to the characteristics of a college specified by charter and to its statutory placement within the world of other organized groups. *Governance* is the codified arrangement whereby a given college systematically assigns to its various constituents responsibilities and rights. Typically, the status of certain groups is linked to the particulars of the legal status of the institution. *Politics* is the process by which individuals and constituencies seek to influence decisions about the distribution of resources. The administrative structure within which a system manages its operations is discussed in chapter 6. The mechanisms described in this chapter, however, are those that determine how successful constituents of the system will be in their competition for recognition and scarce resources.

LEGAL STATUS OF THE COLLEGE

Most, if not all, colleges—whether liberal arts or land grant, junior or teachers—are invested by society with a corporate character. All corporate forms of organization are dependent on their legal status. In the United States, individual state governments maintain more direct control over matters pertaining to the public welfare than does the national government. Corporations, for instance, owe their existence to the states, not to the federal government. Colleges are established in a similar fashion. They are either chartered by special acts of the state legislature or incorporated by the educational or corporation laws of the state. The charter has been defined as a "special enactment by the legislature of the state authorizing the establishment of the institution and defining its powers and privileges," whereas articles of incorporation "consist of an agreement by the founders of the institution, drawn up under the provisions of a general statute."[1] The difference between the two methods of establishment lies in the specificity with which the institution is described. A charter granted by the state legislature applies to one institution only. With articles of incorporation, the legislative action is general and the institution to be established is covered by provisions which were made for other, similar institutions.[2]

Early college charters had the force of a contract and enabled colleges to manage their own affairs. Since 1850, however, when the United States Supreme Court guaranteed the inviolability of the Dartmouth College charter against legislative nullification, states have usually reserved the right to amend or repeal the charter or articles of incorporation of colleges established under general laws of incorporation.

Most colleges and universities established before the educational reform movements of the late nineteenth and early twentieth centuries have their origins in charters. As a result, these institutions may have unique rights or opportunities for development. The charter for Drew University, for instance, issued by the State of New Jersey in 1866, was a permissive document. In time it was invoked by the board of trustees to support the establishment, first, of a seminary, and subsequently, of a college of liberal arts and a graduate school. Should Drew decide at some later time to add other professional schools, it could do so based on the general nature of its charter.

Articles of incorporation granted to privately supported colleges and public institutions founded after 1900 were likely to be more specific and limiting. They were commonly given permission to develop an undergraduate program. If they decided to offer a master's degree, they had to return to the legislature for a revision of their articles of incorporation. In recent years, state departments of higher education have developed policies to avoid excessive duplication of programs, to set minimum standards that must be met before colleges can be incorporated, and to define characteristics that allow an institution be called a "college" or a "university," although definitions can vary across state borders. These state agencies, as well as the Association of Governing Boards of Universities and Colleges, also concern themselves with the role of college trustees.

From the standpoint of legal control, the first and most important distinction between colleges is their origin in either the public or private sector. Public colleges are controlled by a government agency—the state, county or municipal government. The degree of control depends on the nature of the articles of incorporation. Private colleges are generally incorporated as nonprofit charitable organizations and are controlled by a private corporation whose composition and authority are laid down in the college charter. Both types of colleges are exempt from property taxes and exercise certain other powers and rights. These powers are usually vested, under the legislative act or charter that created the college, in a board of trustees. The board owns property, enters into contracts, accepts responsibility for the acts of its officers and employees, and provides the institution with its continuity.

In private colleges, the number of trustees, their mode of selection, and terms of office are usually mandated in the college charter. Ordinarily, the board is self-perpetuating; that is, the trustees themselves select new members as vacancies occur. Denominational colleges usually have representation from the sponsoring church, and many boards, both public and private, have alumni as members. Less typical, and indeed somewhat controversial, is the practice of having a faculty member from the institution, a student, or a representative from a union under contract with the college serve on the board. A few boards of public colleges are elected by the public, but more often they are selected by the governor and confirmed by the state legislature. Terms of office vary from lifetime appointments to a maximum of two successive terms.

State colleges are frequently governed by the state board of education and may not have separate groups of trustees concerned with specific campuses. By and large, the members of boards that control public and private colleges are drawn from the ranks of prominent members of the business community, lawyers, alumni, professional people, foundation executives, educators, civic leaders, and longtime supporters of the college. In the recent past, a good deal of effort has been exerted toward changing the socioeconomic profile of typical college boards by adding women and minority persons to them. At the same time, colleges have increased their expectations about participation of trustees in the life of the community. Such expectations include support for capital campaign contributions at a significant level and support for one or more aspects of campus life through involvement on a trustee committee. Trustees are also expected to be well-informed about the college and able to generate approval and understanding for the mission of the institution in the wider community.

When overseeing college operations, trustees have the authority to draft and put into effect regulations that affect governance, and to define their relations with the college. Generally, such rules are called bylaws and are looked upon as vehicles for implementing the more general grants of authority found in the charter or articles of incorporation. The bylaws contain such information as the official title and address of the college; the college's aims; the names of officers and members of the board as well as their powers and duties; and rules regarding meetings and standing committees. Frequently the bylaws and the charter are printed together and distributed to board members, college officers, and other interested persons. In the absence of bylaws, or in addition to them, there may be official regulations in which the operating responsibility and authority, and procedures for continuing review are clearly defined. A framework for such a document is suggested in the *Statement on Governance of Colleges and Universities* issued jointly by the American Association of University Professors, the American Council on Education, and the Association of Governing Boards of Universities and Colleges.[3]

LEGAL STATUS OF THE LIBRARY

The legal status of the college library is determined, if it is formalized at all, by the charter or articles of incorporation, the bylaws, and the institutional handbook, by whatever name it is known. The charter, as the governing document of the college, is the basic source of authority. However, beyond an occasional reference to the authority of the board of trustees to purchase books, most charters and articles of incorporation have little or nothing to say specifically about the library.

Statements of varying length and complexity on the library appear in the bylaws of some, but by no means all, colleges. The topics covered will generally include the authority of the director of the library as an officer of the college, a general statement of the duties of the library director, a brief statement about the nature of library resources, and perhaps some mention about the methods of appointment of the library director and the professional staff.

GOVERNANCE

In addition to bylaws, most colleges issue a handbook that lists the rules and regulations governing appointment, promotion and retention of faculty. It also describes the standing committees of the faculty and faculty participation in the governance of the college. These provisions are linked to the bylaws. But, while bylaws are the specific province of the board of trustees, the contents of the faculty handbooks are subject to change by the faculty, with the consent of the president and the board of trustees.

What constitutes faculty on a college campus has become a matter of great concern to librarians, many of whom feel that, as professional librarians, they are entitled to faculty status. The troublesome issue of faculty status has generated heated debate among academic librarians, who sometimes even disagree on the meaning of the term.

Faculty status is generally accorded to college and university classroom teachers and brings with it both a structure of rankings and a combination of privileges and responsibilities. Four faculty ranks are commonly assigned to resident faculty at most institutions. They are full, associate and assistant professor, and at the lowest rung, instructor. Salary levels for faculty are based on rank as well as on years of service and quality of work performance. Those holding any of the three professor titles usually have earned a Ph.D., while instructors may be in the process of obtaining one. In most institutions, full and associate professors are tenured, while those in the other ranks are not. To be awarded tenure is to be granted a permanent position. Continuous faculty employment may be abrogated when financial exigencies necessitate college-wide retrenchment or when a faculty member is found guilty of an act of "moral turpitude" or is proved to be no longer performing duties in a satisfactory manner.

In most institutions, judgments about tenurability are made by or before the seventh year of a faculty member's presence on the campus and follow one or two contract renewals. However, the probationary time can vary, and some institutions have adopted "clock-stopping" mechanisms for delaying the determination. Decisions regarding tenure are always made by the president of the institution with approval by the trustees. These decisions, however, are generally based on peer review and a series of recommendations: first by a faculty member's department; second, by a school-wide committee, usually elected by the faculty; and third, by the dean or vice-president/provost. Criteria for granting tenure include quality of teaching, quality of scholarship, and quality of service to the institution and community, with the first two carrying the most weight. Most colleges have formal procedures for appealing decisions on tenure and nonrenewal of contracts. The system of tenure was adopted as, and remains, a protection of intellectual freedom inside and outside of the classroom. Faculty and administrators often lose sight of this original purpose and regard tenure as job security.

Among the privileges associated with faculty status is access to sabbatical and other leaves. The term sabbatical has its origins in the practice of allowing land to remain fallow every seven years in order that it may renew itself. Each institution frames its own sabbatical policy, but commonly faculty members with tenure may anticipate a paid leave of absence for at least one semester every seventh year. Grants, fellowships, and research funds are more accessible to those with faculty status than they are to other members of the academic community. Other characteristics of faculty status include: active involvement in campus governance and curricular affairs; voting memberships in permanent committees of the faculty; and participation in the faculty councils and senates of an institution.

Academic status, a term adopted by some institutions to describe those who are not primarily classroom teachers but who are involved in the educational program, usually carries some, but not all, faculty privileges. However, faculty rank, tenure, and readier access to sabbaticals and research development money may or may not be part of the package. Traditions and practices vary among colleges, as do definitions of faculty rank, faculty status, and full faculty status. Rank often means the use of titles but not full privileges, while status means titles are not used. Full usually means equal to teaching faculty in all respects.

FACULTY STATUS FOR LIBRARIANS

Good arguments have been mounted on both sides of the debate about status for librarians. Outspoken advocates have been known to shift positions over time. Former opponents of tenure for librarians have become advocates. Still others recommend a middle course, accepting some elements of faculty and/or academic status for librarians while rejecting others. In 1974, the Association of College and Research Libraries and the American Association of University Professors issued a joint statement asserting that the correct status for all librarians working in colleges and universities is full faculty status. Many who endorsed the statement have since recanted or withdrawn their support. A revision of that policy has recently been issued.[4]

Those who favor faculty status for librarians maintain that it ensures they will be recognized as equal partners in the academic community and as members of the instructional and research staffs of the institution. Different titles, salaries, schedules, and methods of selection and evaluation cause librarians to be regarded as something different, and, inevitably, as inferior to teaching faculty. The contribution that librarians make to the educational process is, after all, intellectual in nature. It is the product of considerable formal education, includes training at the graduate level, and culminates in a terminal degree. Librarians perform a teaching and research role by instructing students formally and informally, as well as by advising faculty in scholarly pursuits. In addition, faculty status permits librarians themselves to become productive scholars because it gives them access to grants and sabbatical leaves.

Among the other dividends of faculty status among librarians is the emergence of a collegial model of library governance, one that permits participative management and peer participation in personnel decisions. Hiring becomes a committee effort, and promotion and tenure are based on criteria accepted by faculty both inside and outside the library. Further, aligning with the faculty, particularly if they are unionized, gives librarians bargaining leverage. Finally, in the same way that tenure ensures individual professors the right to speak out on matters they consider important, tenure for librarians helps to protect librarians against capricious decisions, enables them to criticize the administration with impunity, and permits them to exercise purely professional judgment when purchasing materials they believe are appropriate to their collections.

Arguments mounted by opponents of faculty status are often based on the premise that librarianship is a different profession from that practiced by classroom teachers and, therefore should be measured by a different yardstick. Opponents see the goals of teaching faculty as presenting in systematic fashion a coherent viewpoint on a given portion of reality. They view librarians as bringing order from chaos and making various bodies of truth available in a useful fashion. Librarians, they contend, should be librarians, not ersatz professors, and should be rewarded on the basis of an independent, self-reliant position. They should be judged by standards that relate to what they do, not to what someone else does. Tenure, they point out, is generally granted on the basis of teaching, research, professional activity, service to the community, and general usefulness, often in that order. Librarians considered for tenure must either have these priorities reordered or be granted status based on different, perhaps lesser performance when it comes to research, or reorder their own priorities and work schedules. Many who question faculty status have witnessed the extraordinary pressures on librarians aspiring to tenure under circumstances requiring them to maintain full library schedules, and to publish and teach. The opponents of faculty status also question the motives of those who support it, suggesting that prestige and social benefits may be the primary reasons for its being sought.

Traditionally, library directors at colleges were the only library staff members to hold full faculty status or even a partial form of faculty rank. Other librarians had no formal access to participation in the academic life of an institution. However, more recently, some colleges that grant faculty status to librarians are loath to include directors, whom they consider administrators. In yet other institutions, library directors hold positions as chairs of library departments and on that basis are included among the ranks of faculty. Newer colleges with collective bargaining agreements, colleges with a strong history of participative management, publicly supported colleges, and a bare majority of the high-quality liberal arts colleges have a governance approach that seems to favor the inclusion of librarians in the faculty, albeit with some reservations. While practices vary, the full integration of all librarians in the teaching faculty is relatively rare, even when they share nomenclature and are awarded tenure. Distinctions between faculty and librarians are found in the way in which promotion criteria are articulated and implemented, in relative financial rewards, in granting of leaves, and in providing opportunities for research and education support. In a telling survey of fifty-nine college library directors by Kathleen Moretto Spenser, twenty-three indicated that their staffs have faculty status, twenty maintained that their status was comparable to faculty, but only eight reported that tenure was available to librarians.[5]

ROLE OF THE COLLEGE ADMINISTRATION

More essential even than status considerations, perhaps, is the need to articulate and codify the positions of librarians in the bylaws or in the faculty handbook. It would seem self-evident that the library—involving as it does considerable responsibility for funds and personnel—should have a clearly expressed code of policy or governance. In fact, because libraries are so infrequently mentioned in an institution's official documents, control and governance are largely determined by tradition, precedent, and personalities. Unfortunately, the tradition of the library in the college history is often not an exalted one, and librarians are seldom regarded as influential policy makers. More typically, they are viewed as quiet and able administrators, in charge of worthy and necessary domains, but not among the principal campus policy makers. Robert Munn's comment, made in 1968, is still apt:

"Librarians are not normally part of either the administrative inner circle itself or the select group of faculty oligarchies and entrepreneurs whose views carry great weight. They are thus excluded from the real decision-making process in the institution."[6] Among the real dangers in depending entirely on unwritten customs for library governance are confusion and disagreement. Moreover, informal agreements on library policies do not necessarily remain effective when there is a change in either the college administration or the library directorship. A clear-cut statement that describes the relationship of the library and librarians to the other parts of the college community and provides for appropriately shared responsibility and activity among them will serve to prevent misunderstanding.

The college administration's unique, as well as most obvious, role is to define the library director's authority and responsibility and to identify the director in the web of organization and services of the institution. Among the matters that need formal codification, or at least guidelines, are the flow of authority from the president to the library director, the control of funds for the purchase of library materials, the establishment and administration of departmental libraries, the control of the location of library materials, the selection of the staff, and other similar concerns. Because library directors must deal with and exert pressure on a variety of constituencies—deans, departmental chairpersons, faculty, students, administrators—they must have some recourse to formal documents that clarify issues of governance. Every library director should keep a file in which records of substantive discussions or policy changes in any of these areas are kept. The file can document for an incumbent director why certain practices are in force. Without such a record, library directors and administrators, both old and new, must rely on oral histories which may be either inaccurate or ambiguous. Custom and trust are terribly important on a college campus, but it is also well to have some documentation.

POLITICS

Unlike their nineteenth-century predecessors, few directors today report directly to the president of the college. The majority do, however, report to the chief academic officer—the dean of the college, the provost, or the academic vice president. Library directors with reporting relationships at this level have some regular opportunities to participate in institutional policy decisionmaking. If the director holds the rank of dean, and meets with other deans, the potential for influence is even greater. Unfortunately, most library directors do not meet formally more than once or twice a year with the person to whom they report. When meetings are set, it is more often than not during times of budget review or budget development. However, in optimal situations, meetings are far more frequent. Weekly meetings give evidence of support for the library's centrality and offer opportunities to foster collaborative projects. While few librarians report directly to the president, access to the president's office is not difficult on most college campuses.

In addition, many directors see presidents socially. One college library director invites the president and his wife to dinner once a semester to create an informal environment in which views about the college and the library's role in it can be exchanged. Other library directors seek informal campus opportunities to nurture their relationships with faculty and administrators. Serving on a search committee, participating in an accreditation self-study, or playing a role in a long-range or strategic planning effort helps to identify the library director or staff member as part of the academic community. Visibility in the informal and formal life of the college is important. The process of gathering support for the library is ongoing and requires strong political and interpersonal skills. Librarians are not successful, nor are their libraries good, simply because the books are ordered and shelved expeditiously. Librarians are successful, in part, because they have opened channels of communication with their constituents and have developed mutual respect and understanding with them.

Membership in standing committees of the faculty presents yet another opportunity for participation in policymaking for librarians. Most colleges have faculty committees—both appointed, and elected by the teaching staff—to advise the president on policy and practical matters; to consider curriculum; to decide on cases of reappointment, promotion, and tenure; to evaluate faculty requests for research funds; to plan public events; and to award honorary degrees, among other tasks. These committees vary in importance from campus to campus. Nonetheless, it is not difficult to identify which committees are prestigious and include faculty who are well-respected and influential at any given college. Elected committees tend to be more highly regarded than appointed ones; those that deal with items of concern to the president, those that accept responsibility for the conditions of employment of their peers, and those that consider curricular, budget, and planning matters are generally important.

While librarians who hold faculty status may sit on these

committees, too often they are overlooked when committee assignments are made. Particularly shortsighted is the nonappointment of librarians, even in an ex officio capacity, to the committees responsible for curriculum decisions. Ignoring the library when considering new courses carries the danger that the library holdings may be insufficient to support the subjects being offered. Despite their exclusion from committees, librarians should be aware of the pecking order—the relative status of serving on one or another of the committees. Courting faculty members whose opinion is respected by their colleagues is not unseemly behavior. Individuals are thought of as leaders when they have something to say that resonates with the opinions of others who become their followers. This is equally true on a college campus. Library directors are well advised to listen carefully to those faculty members who are elected to the important standing committees, who are chosen by the administration for ad hoc, long-range planning committees, or who appointed to committees to search for high-level administrators.

Building a core of library supporters among the faculty is facilitated by the enlightened self-interest of those professors who are particularly interested in having resources available for their own work as scholars. Publicizing new library resources to the faculty therefore becomes an important means to recruit library supporters. Faculty in departments with strong majors whose students use library materials are seen as particularly valuable allies. A recent informal study of library directors revealed that although support for the library was found most often among history and English faculty, no generalizations about the degree of support from other disciplines could be made.[7] On one campus, the library's strongest friends might be found in the chemistry department and on another, among the political scientists. In any given year, there are also a few vocal student leaders who gain power by virtue of their ability to sway the opinions of other students. They, too, should be identified and kept informed about the library.

LIBRARY COMMITTEE

The one faculty committee on which the library director is assured membership is, of course, the library committee. Virtually all colleges have, as part of their permanent faculty committee structure, a committee that considers the role, function, and operation of the library. With proper members, the library committee can play an invaluable liaison role on the campus. While some librarians are emphatic in their praise of library committees, others are openly skeptical about their value. The division in opinion stems from the fact that, like almost everything else on a college campus, the library committee is a product of its environment. The degree to which it is thought important or influential will determine who is willing to serve on it. On one campus, it may be composed of influential and interested faculty members. On others, it may be seen as a way to meet a community service commitment without having to do much work. The size and composition of library committees varies from campus to campus. They may be large or small depending on whether they are designed to represent departments or divisions. Members of the committee are selected in one of three ways: appointment by the president, appointment by the chief academic officer, or, most commonly, appointment by the faculty—either directly or through a faculty committee on committees. Combinations of these methods are found in some colleges.

Members serve from one to five years, though there are occasional instances in which the term of office appears to be indefinite. A plan that ensures continuity without sterility provides for rotating membership on the committee, with one or two new professors replacing long-serving ones each year. Student representation on the committee can give both the library director and the committee a better understanding of how students view the library—hours, regulations, undergraduate collections—than they can obtain from other sources.

Library committees are almost always advisory and not administrative. Their function is to consider matters of general library policy, how best to develop library resources, and the most effective means by which the library program can be integrated with other academic activities of the college. While their clout is limited by their advisory capacity, members' advice and recommendations on policy questions as well as on matters of administration can be invaluable. The professional staff may set library policy, but undergirding collegial politics and practice is the assumption that others have a need to review the implications of that policy. That is the function of the library committee. If the library committee is seen as a rubber stamp, it is unlikely to be effective either in advising on library matters or in interpreting them to the faculty. Some directors find it exceedingly difficult to refrain from dominating committee deliberations. For this reason, among others, a librarian should not serve as chair of the library committee. Some have suggested, perhaps facetiously, that the librarian act as secretary to the committee, thereby making excessive participation more difficult. However, no matter who keeps the minutes, they should be carefully kept and widely distributed. Routinely routing copies to the president, provost, deans, and chief business officer ensures full access to any information about recommendations, resolutions or other actions that have been considered by the library committee.

The liaison role is one of the most important functions of the library committee. On the one hand, the library serves the entire college, and its actions effect the entire community; on the other, the library is a tight, complex agency whose inner workings are largely unknown to those who use it. Library administrators utilize the library committee to keep themselves fully informed about new educational policies, new courses, new instructors, and new plans for campus development. They also depend on the committee to act as their interpreter to the wider community, to explain how it operates and why it follows particular procedures. The committee's Janus-like relationship to the community and the library can help to prevent misunderstandings and to keep the library from being isolated. Historians, mathematicians, and professors of English, all taking their turn serving on a library committee, gaining familiarity with the library's management and utilization, learning why it makes certain decisions, constitute a knowledgeable corps of faculty members in a position to inform their colleagues about the library. Often, these former members become the library's strongest supporters as they serve on other committees that affect the library.

The success of the library committee is determined by the attitudes toward it of the director and of the faculty members who serve on it. The committee members must be genuinely interested in the development of the library as a whole and not merely in their departmental relationships to it. The director must have faith in the usefulness of the library committee, must be willing to share information with it, and must have the patience to let the committee work its way through library matters. The agenda items may be crucial to the interest that faculty members sustain in the committee. If they are called upon to discuss inconsequential details, they are unlikely to show much enthusiasm. However, neither will their interest be piqued by endless discussions of unrealistic five-year plans that never reach fulfillment.

The distinction between policy determination and administrative matters is best ignored by the library committee. Its central mission is to improve the library's effectiveness in the educational program of a college and to collaborate on the development of policies and practices to meet these goals. Some of the chief topics that appear on library committee agendas are: budgets; automation; allocation of book funds to departments; policies and practices of bibliographic instruction; library resources; campus satisfaction with the library; duplication of reserve materials; policies on purchase of audio-visual materials; periodicals; gift policies; staffing practices; enlarging, remodeling, or constructing a new building; circulation rules and regulations; departmental collections; and staff status.

SUMMARY

Each college has a defined legal status. Description of the role and responsibilities of the library director and of other librarians may be sparse in the college bylaws, but some official publications such as the faculty handbook or the college personnel policy manual document their positions and duties. Tradition most often governs the important relationships between the library and its constituents. However, important interpretations of policy or practices should be noted and kept on file to prevent misunderstanding, or to educate a new president or dean. In addition to the formal structures, librarians should develop informal communication networks of support and information which can be utilized both routinely and in times of emergency changes on the campus.

NOTES

1. Floyd W. Reeves et al., *The Liberal Arts College* (Chicago: University of Chicago Press, 1932), 62.

2. Reeves et al., *Liberal Arts,* 62.

3. American Association of University Professors, *Bulletin* 52 (Winter 1966): 375-79.

4. ACRL, "Guidelines for Academic Status for College and University Libraries," *College and Research Libraries News* 51 (March 1990): 245-46.

5. Kathleen Moretto Spenser, unpublished survey, September 5, 1989.

6. Robert Munn, "The Bottomless Pit," *College and Research Libraries News* 21 (January 1968): 51; Dennis P. Carrigan, "The Political Economies of the Academic Library," *College and Research Libraries* 49 (July 1988): 325-31.

7. Caroline Coughlin and Alice Gertzog, unpublished survey of sixty directors of liberal arts college libraries, October 1989.

Chapter 6

ORGANIZATION OF THE LIBRARY

In the early history of American colleges, administrative organization was hardly needed. There was a faculty, and from its ranks one person was selected as president. The faculty was small and the president the only officer with executive authority. As the college grew, the first positions to be differentiated from that of the president were those of librarian and registrar. Both were chosen from the faculty, and the librarian generally held that post on a part-time basis. Since all records of the institution, including student courses and grades, were kept by the registrar, his office became the natural center for institutional planning. Gradually, as the college increased in size and complexity, these record-keeping duties were divorced from planning, and a new academic executive position was created with the title of dean. Generally speaking, the academic duties of the dean and the executive tasks carried out as deputy to the president described only part of that position's functions. The dean almost always also fulfilled responsibilities related to the personal problems of students.

ORGANIZATION OF THE COLLEGE

As college student bodies became larger, a further division of labor occurred. New administrative offices were created to oversee such problems as health care, business management, and the physical plant. Each officer of these new departments reported directly to the president, until, finally, the number of people with direct access was greater than time available. The president could no longer provide adequate time for the kind of consultation necessary for effective academic administration. Administrative overload then precipitated the creation of new reporting relationships. What finally evolved was a pyramidal structure, one now followed by virtually every college in the country. Variations abound, of course, depending on the nature of the institution and its size. In recent years, the pressure on college presidents, particularly in private institutions, to raise funds has resulted in the designation of someone other than the president to serve as the college's chief academic officer. Often this is the vice president for academic affairs, the provost, or the dean of the college, although other titles are sometimes used. While structures may vary from institution to institution, college organizations generally resemble that in figure 4.

Nomenclature, too, may vary. The provost/dean of the faculty is as likely to be called vice president of academic affairs, or vice president of instruction. The treasurer may be the chief financial officer. The head of development may be called the vice president of institutional development. It is customary for the library director to report to a provost or academic vice president, but this, too, differs by institution. The director may report directly to the president. The implications of reporting relationships, particularly as they relate to librarians, were considered in the previous chapter in conjunction with the discussion of governance and politics.

Figures 4 and 5 represent organizational structures of a private and a public institution. They describe the administrative structure of many public colleges in the United States today. A dotted line represents a staff or advisory relationship; a solid one, the chain of command relationship. In each of these figures, the board of trustees is the ultimate authority, although in the case of figure 5 there is a state commissioner of higher education in the employ of state government who also exercises authority over the institution. The president is accountable to the trustees, while the library director reports to the chief academic officer of the institution.

Experiments abound. Franklin and Marshall College has combined the position of library director and director of academic computing into an assistant vice president position some years and in other years kept them separate, with the decisions based on campus priorities and personnel realities. In the mid-1980s at both Rutgers and Columbia Universities, the positions of library director and director of computing Services were combined. A single person, a librarian with the rank of vice president was named to oversee both operations and report to the president at each university. In 1996, Columbia University maintained that model, while Rutgers University had two distinct positions.

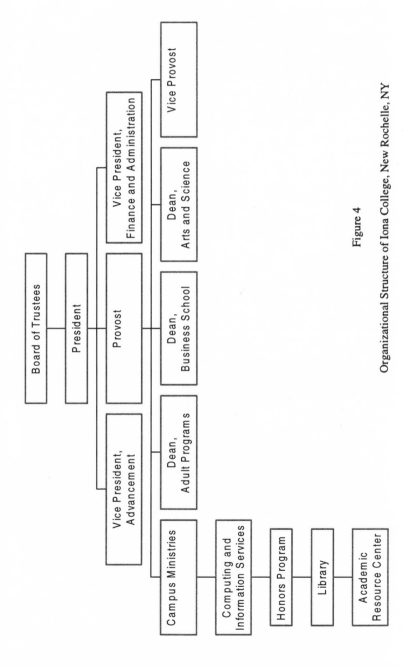

Figure 4

Organizational Structure of Iona College, New Rochelle, NY

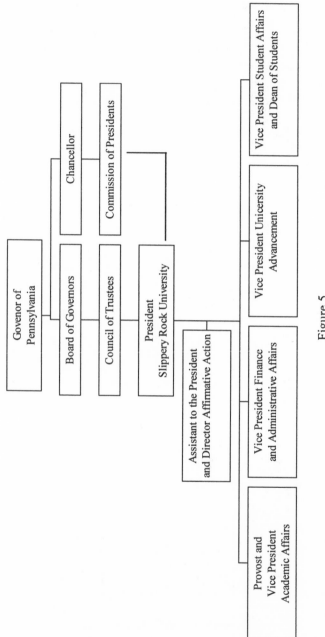

Figure 5

Organization of Slippery Rock University, Penn.
The University and the State System of Higher Education

Connecticut College, Gettysburg College and St. John's University (Collegeville, Minnesota) are three institutions that have modified their organizational structures in recent years to accommodate the integration of academic computing and library services. In two of the three situations, the person given the responsibility for directing the combined program had been the library director at the college or university.

The library director as administrator must be intimately acquainted with the pattern of administrative organization on the campus in order to deal effectively with the management team. The director usually works closely with: the campus personnel director, to recruit and reward library staff; the head of the physical plant, to repair and maintain library facilities; the dean, to insure coordination of the library and academic programs; the directors of academic and administrative computing, to ensure smooth integration of new technologies; the director of financial aid, to arrange for work-study student assistants; the business manager, to monitor and reconcile the library's finances, and the development office, to attract gifts.

THE LIBRARY AS AN ORGANIZATION

All organizations exhibit some similar characteristics. Before discussing how college libraries have been structured, how they are currently configured, and how they may be organized in the future, it would be well to look at the traditional hallmarks of an organization as they relate to libraries. The following description is borrowed from Richard Hall:

> An organization is a collectivity with a relatively identifiable boundary, a normative order, authority ranks, communications systems. This collectivity exists on a relatively continuous basis in an environment and engages in activities that are usually related to a goal or set of goals.[1]

College libraries, as we have said, exist within a parent body. Like the administrative arm of the larger institutions, they are generally organized as hierarchies and have levels of authority and responsibility. Their aims and goals should be reflected in their organizational structure, which, in turn, should serve as the vehicle by which choices are made about how operations and staff are arranged, coordinated, and integrated. Structural arrangements should never be immutable but, rather, should be available to be manipulated as required to help achieve new or changed goals and objectives. Two of the most important duties of a library director are to clarify for the staff and for the college the library's role, and to select appropriate means to carry it out.

Each of the library's constituencies may have different expectations of it. Faculty members may believe that the library's chief function is to further their research and, therefore, deem collection development to be the library's most important activity. College administrators, on the other hand, may stress managerial concerns and concentrate on the library's ability to acquire, organize, and disseminate information efficiently and effectively. And, finally, students may assume that the library's preeminent role is to assist them in locating and securing materials, particularly those placed on reserve by their instructors, or perhaps to be there as a study hall twenty-four hours a day.

Obviously, all of these expectations are legitimate and must be satisfied, at least to some extent, by the library. The degree of importance attached to each group's interests by the library director, together with existing institutional norms and traditions, shape the organizational structure of the library.

FORMULATING GOALS AND OBJECTIVES

Formulating goals and objectives for the library is an important task, one that should be accomplished regularly, at least every three years. They should be crafted with the active participation of students, faculty, administrators and library staff. A library director may serve as the primary drafter and then ask the library committees, both staff and faculty, to assist in the shaping of the finished document; or work may begin at the department level in the library and move upward and out. Goals and objectives not only help to determine staff structure, but serve to explain to the campus what the library is trying to achieve. There are additional, very important reasons for formulating goals and objectives.

1. The act of articulating goals and objectives is, in itself, a consciousness-raising experience. If, after their formulation, they are banished to a closet shelf to gather dust, the exercise will still have been worth the effort, given the heightened understanding of the library and its

role in the educational process that formulating them has provided.

2. Goals and objectives can be used to rationalize staffing patterns. Individual roles and activity groups can be compared with the objectives to ensure that harmony exists among them.

3. A publicly available list of goals acts as a contract with the college community. If it has been negotiated with interested parties, it can serve to reconcile the vested interests of all of the library's constituencies.

4. The list has importance as a public relations document. Any college library faces heavy competition for college dollars. Obtaining funds for a department on a college campus may involve engaging in the intellectual equivalent of warfare, a battle in which each participant tries to make the best case and gain adequate leverage. A formulated set of objectives helps to solidify and explain the centrality of the library to the college's mission.

The first set of objectives is often formulated as part of a planning process. Any number of guidebooks are available that provide directions on how to do it, almost in cookbook fashion.[2] The specific procedure followed is always modified to meet the needs of a particular institution.

The planning process generally begins with a statement of the mission of the library (or the college). It is followed by a community survey including an environmental scan and demographic analysis. Depending on time and staff constraints, some or all the information generated by responses to the questions posed in chapter 4 would be included. The next step is to articulate the goals of the library as related to the goals of the colleges. Based on these goals, objectives are formulated. Objectives differ from goals in that objectives are less general and always measurable. For instance, while one of the goals of a college library might be to "create information-literate students,"—the objective might read, "College X will offer twelve bibliographic instruction courses to three hundred students during the fall semester of the academic year 1992." It should be noted that missions, goals, aims, and objectives do not always share the same meaning in library literature. Goals and objectives are sometimes used interchangeably. So, too, are goals and aims. The final step in the planning process is evaluation. During this time, an assessment is made of how well the library has met its objectives. Since the process is circular, it begins again. The mission is reaffirmed, any changes in the community are noted, the goals are reconsidered to see if they still reflect accurately what the library seeks to accomplish, and the objectives are reformed or changed as needed.

The following statement of goals and objectives (figure 6) was prepared by the Upjohn Library at Kalamazoo College and contains the concerns common to most college libraries:

Upjohn Library, Kalamazoo College
Statement of Goals and Objectives

Mission
The mission of the Upjohn Library is to provide services and resources to meet the present and future scholarly and informational needs of the Kalamazoo College community, and in so far as possible, to share these resources with the broader scholarly community.

Continuing Goals
1. To provide a collection of information resources which meet most of the curricular, informational and research needs of the College community.
2. To organize and control the collection for maximum utilization.
3. To maintain the collection in usable physical condition and conserve the material for future generations of users.
4. To organize, monitor, and evaluate library services and procedures to assure the effective and efficient utilization of funds available now and in the future.
5. To provide bibliographic aids and assistance in identifying, locating, and using information resources, including those not available in the Kalamazoo College collection, but which are needed to support the instructional and research programs of the College.
6. To provide facilities and equipment for the storage and use of information resources.
7. To maintain and further develop a highly capable

library staff through systematic programs of career development and effective utilization of individual talents to fulfill the library's mission and support its objectives.

8. To maintain effective administration planning services.

9. To maintain a close and meaningful working relationship with administrative and academic departments, academic planning groups, and the user communities, to assure effective development of library services consistent with objectives and programs of the College, and to advise the College as to requirements and costs of these resources.

10. To promote the use of the library and information resources.

11. To continually investigate opportunities to increase services and access to collections beyond the College through cooperative programs with other libraries, library organizations, and information retrieval systems.

12. To maintain constant exploration of professional and technological developments with a constant view to applicability for Kalamazoo College.

13. To insure continued development and utilization of those collections of a specialized or pre-eminent nature which are distinctive to Kalamazoo College and which are of recognized and national interest.[3]

Figure 6

Statement of Goals and Objectives Upjohn Library
Kalamazoo College, Kalamazoo, Mich.

A timeline chart from Occidental College (figure 7) illustrates the relationship between goals, objectives, and schedules.

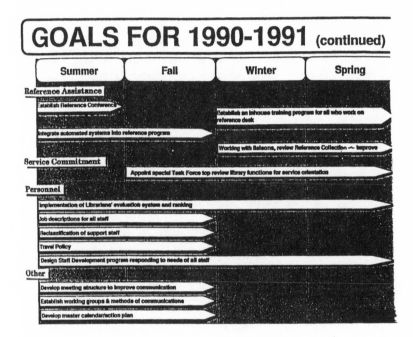

Figure 7

Goals for 1990-91, Mary Norton Clapp Library,
Occidental College, Los Angeles, Calif.

ORGANIZATIONAL STRUCTURE

As mentioned earlier, the organizational structure of the library should be a product of its mission and goals, and its organizational chart a description of the functional relationships among job title holders. However, organizational structure is often a reflection of patterns of behavior that have developed gradually over time as adaptations to the skills of staff members. Individual strengths and weaknesses account for crucial differences in an organization's success, particularly in relation to the relatively small groups represented by the college library staff. The wise administrator selects the right people and lets them grow according to their individual talents and interests. On the other hand, there are activities that all college libraries must accomplish. These would include: collection management, acquisitions, cataloging, circulation, reference services, and library instruction. What follows is a brief overview of the major tasks involved in each of these activities.

Collection management or development involves evaluation and selection of materials to be added to the library, evaluation and weeding out of materials no longer useful, preservation of library holdings, and strategies for ensuring rational growth and curriculum support.

Acquisitions includes ordering materials, monitoring deliveries, and approving payments. Among the duties are: searching files for ownership; collecting bibliographic information; selecting suppliers; ordering and checking deliveries; initiating claims for unreceived materials.

Cataloging entails recording, describing, and indexing the holdings of a library. The number and kind of access points for retrieving each item are determined and established, and the quality control of all bibliographic records monitored.

Circulation encompasses activities revolving around the flow of library materials; that is, managing the removal and return of items to and from their shelf locations.

Reference services involves helping users locate, retrieve and otherwise gain access to information.

Library instruction refers to teaching students how to use the library and its materials.

Special collections, archives and audio-visual services may be called out separately in larger libraries.

Special collections includes those materials deemed rare by virtue of their great age, subject focus, printing history, or, in a more practical approach, particularly high price.

Archives refers to the historical collection of official and semiofficial records of the college. They are organized by issuing agency and housed separately, often under the control of the library.

Audio-visual services, also known as media services or instructional media, encompasses the in-house production and classroom distribution of films, videos and audio materials. The production and distribution function may be separate entities on a given campus, and either or both may be under the control of the library.

College libraries today adopt many different organizational structures depending on their size, institutional environment, and available space, among other factors. The size of the campus and the distances that library users must traverse in order to reach the library may determine, for instance, the extent to which departmental libraries are desirable. Automation, too, accounts for differing organizational structures among college libraries and also contributes to fluctuating conditions and rapid change. The opportunity for altered arrangements presented by the new technology, as well as discontent with current operating structures, has spawned numerous suggestions for reorganizing academic libraries. A number of proposals for change are considered here, following a description and discussion of how academic libraries are currently organized.

In the small college library, there is either no elaborate organization, or the library has organized its work around the particular skills of a few staff members. There is very little departmentalization, and duties are assigned to the person who has the time or who performs them best. While organization in a small or medium-sized library often represents adaptation to individual capabilities, the duties assigned to an individual staff member should be closely related, if possible, and that person should be asked to report to only one supervisor. Adaptation in the small library can result in effective service patterns and a well-functioning operation. On the other hand, it can produce a dysfunctional, unbalanced institution with some staff severely overburdened and others underutilized.

As the library grows larger and there are more than three or four staff members, the common pattern is consciously to divide areas of responsibility. Six bases on which libraries are organized have been identified.[4] Most college libraries contain examples of each of these bases of organization. They are (1) function; (2) activity or process; (3) clientele; (4) geography; (5) subject; and (6) form of material. A functional arrangement would be the traditional organization depicted in figure 8. Activity or process as a basis of organization may be illustrated by such units as photocopying and book repair. An organization based on form of material would include separate departments for serials, documents, and collections such as manuscripts, rare books, and other materials that require special protection. Department libraries are often formed on the basis of location and/or subject. The form of information, particularly information generated by computers and audio-visually, has resulted in widespread departmentalization. Few college libraries, for instance, are currently without a media department although this too may change with recent attention to content regardless of format. Figure 9 depicts a typical library with a structure that mixes function, format, and location.

The organizational chart fulfills two important purposes. It provides a structure for job titles, and it describes the relationship between them. In this way, the areas of responsibility and authority are delineated. The current organizational chart of most college libraries reflects a structure that is hierarchical and crafted along predominantly traditional functional lines. Technical services, reference services and circulation generally have their own departments (see figure 8). Some libraries combine circulation and reference services into a single unit and maintain a two-part, or bifurcated, structure composed of public services and collection management services (see figure 10).

Unfortunately, it is the rare college library director who maintains an up-to-date chart of the library's internal organization, complete with staff assignments. Most charts are created at the request of a new administrator or at the time of a self-study for accreditation and, librarians contend, only capture the reality of a given moment in an organization's development. They cite lack of available time as an excuse for not maintaining a current organizational chart. But there is also widespread reluctance to accept a chart as an accurate reflection of reporting relationships. Dotted and solid lines may indicate ideal advisory, coordinating, or authority and responsibility paths, but they do not reveal the quality or frequency of exchanges between individuals who hold titles. Two organizational charts that duplicate each other may describe entirely different organizations. In one, a library director may meet frequently with the provost and have an excellent working relationship with that officer. In another, the provost may let a year go by without seeking a formal meeting with the director, and the library may suffer.

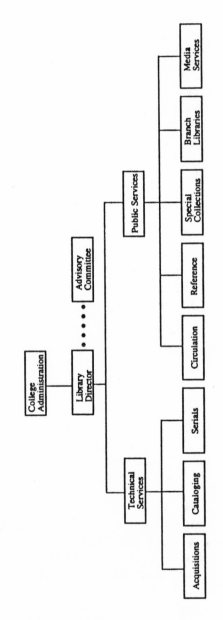

Figure 8

Organizational Chart, Typical College Library

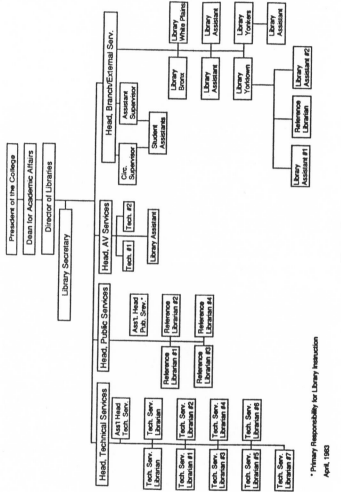

Figure 9

Organizational chart, Mercy College Library, Dobbs Ferry, NY

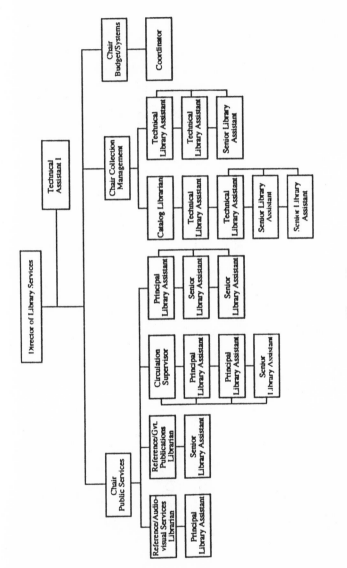

Figure 10

Organizational Chart, Ramapo College Library, Mahwah, N.J.

Organizational structures of college libraries have tended to imitate those of university libraries. Job titles are duplicated, and attempts are made to follow similar internal operations. Critics contend, however, that college libraries should not try to copy university libraries. The objectives and roles of the two differ, and the patterns that suit university libraries may be inhibiting to new services and professional staff development in a college library environment.[5] Among the major differences between college and university libraries is the absence of staff specialist positions. College libraries do not have the resources to employ personnel librarians, library budget officers, or even, in many cases, system librarians. In a college library, the director is responsible for these areas as well as for the general tasks of planning and leading the overall library program. While university library directors focus much of their energies on promoting and explaining the library to constituents outside the library, relying on associate librarians to administer the library, college library directors do not have that luxury. They are charged with speaking for the library to the outside community, but they also bear day-to-day responsibility for administering their libraries. It is this dual role—the integration of external and internal responsibilities on a manageable scale—that has attracted librarians to the college environment. The size of the operation also has a bearing on their sense of satisfaction since work in a smaller organization permits a greater degree of personal interaction with coworkers and users. Not only do college library directors and librarians find the work exciting and personally satisfying, but they also consider their potential influence and impact on higher education to be substantial.

DEPARTMENTAL AND DIVISIONAL LIBRARIES

One of the most controversial and difficult problems which college librarians have faced has been the library's relationship to certain collections housed in other places on the campus. Early colleges were composed of a single building that served as a dormitory and provided classrooms, offices, and a library. As the campus grew from one building to several, it was common for libraries to develop within each one. With further departmentalization, these libraries grew and often became the fiefdoms of the faculty members associated with the departments where they were housed. It was not unusual to find numerous small department libraries on a college campus. They were frequently administered and maintained by academic departments.

During the last three decades, there has been a major push to divest campuses of satellite libraries. The action was predicated on both pedagogical and management concerns. Not surprisingly, the effort to eliminate departmental libraries provoked a storm of protest from faculty and resulted in political crises on many campuses. One library director at a Southern university who disbanded departmental libraries was burned in effigy by faculty and graduate students.

The issues involved in decentralization-centralization, divisionalism and departmentalization are complex and have been subjected to continual debate. Good arguments for all positions can be offered. With centralization, there is less need to duplicate texts and records. Moreover, material is made available to the entire student body, rather than only to the majors. In this way, overlapping and interdisciplinary documents are not located in a variety of sites. Better organization, coordination, and control over materials is possible, and planning for the development and balancing of collections is facilitated. Housing all materials in a main library assures better services to the public by providing: (1) longer hours of access; (2) more agreement on rules governing libraries; and (3) the services of a professional staff to do justice to the collection. In addition, the central library becomes a meeting ground for students and faculty from all disciplines, thus discouraging parochial attitudes among disciplines and departments. Finally, centralizing improves security control over materials and ensures that items requiring preservation are given appropriate treatment.

But many faculty prefer libraries in close proximity to where they teach and do their work. This gives them unlimited access to library materials and, often, more awareness of their existence. Research into library use has repeatedly shown that, based on the principle of least effort, use is a function of accessibility, which in turn is defined as distance, time, and/or familiarity. Departmental libraries may promote library use. In addition, centralized libraries require larger physical plants than may be available. Eliminating departmental libraries may therefore represent a costlier change than many colleges are prepared to undertake. It is often contended that centralized libraries provide more uniform service across disciplines. However, even advocates admit that it is not always as good for particular patron groups. Many librarians without strong science backgrounds rely on faculty to help students use departmental science collections. With centralization, a subject deficiency within the staff may become more pronounced and critical. While it is true that centralization reduces library costs, it is also true that it may increase user costs and be more expensive in the long run.

In the 1960s, a number of academic libraries began to embrace a divisional system of organization, with humanities, social sciences, and science having separate rooms or even buildings. This compromise plan exhibits advantages of both departmental and centralized libraries, although it retains some of the drawbacks of both. A divisional approach characterizes the curriculum of many colleges, and libraries so structured are able to relate most directly to the program of instruction. Librarians who administer humanities collections, for instance, will grow to know their particular clientele, thereby offering better service. Interdisciplinary problems are reduced by having materials together. On the other hand, divisional libraries are more expensive than functional ones. A larger and more varied staff is required, and finding divisional subject specialists is difficult. This organization may lead to disputes over particular kinds of materials, and area studies specialists will have trouble using the collection.

In recent years, a number of the leading liberal arts colleges have chosen to build a science division library when the library became overcrowded, rather than expand the main building. This decision may result in gaining an additional twenty years of service for the old building and could save the institution a considerable sum of money. Scientists are more successful in obtaining their own library than members of other disciplines because their need to have materials placed in closer proximity to laboratories seems more compelling. In addition, foundations have been more willing to support requests for science libraries than they have other kinds of applications. Within the past few years, Franklin and Marshall College and Bowdoin College have followed the lead of Smith, Earlham, Knox, Wellesley, Wesleyan, Swarthmore, and Colby by building or establishing separate science libraries.

Institutions that decide to support, or tolerate, departmental or divisional libraries should put into place a set of controls to monitor and limit their growth. The first hedge against their proliferation is a statement of policy on departmental collections and libraries, endorsed by the college administration and faculty either through the library committee or via departmental chairs. The second defense is to limit the funds available to satellite facilities and to discourage fundraising for them by departments. The third, and most important, way to discourage the proliferation of departmental libraries is to provide good service in the main library.

TECHNOLOGY AND ORGANIZATIONAL CHANGE

Ironically, many of the arguments in favor of centralization disappear with the arrival of new methods of document storage and retrieval, and many observers predict a new "decentralization" of libraries. Online systems are "distance-independent." Online public access catalogs and bibliographic databases are accessible through any computer and are therefore not limited to a particular location. With the addition of electronic-mail systems, materials can be brought directly into the office of any faculty member or the dorm room of any student. Staff, too, are less rooted to a particular site. Catalogers need not be in proximity to the catalog to accomplish their work, nor do those who place orders or check in serials. As the campus is increasingly "wired," access becomes less limited to place and more dependent on the user's knowledge of how to gain entry and how to evaluate the information once retrieved.

Although he did not use the term *virtual library*, Hugh Atkinson predicted, in 1984, that the organizational pattern of the academic library of the future is likely to be a decentralized one:

> one can already see the beginnings of new pressures and new organizational patterns with the advent of high density, optical digital discs, carbon fiber optics, and satellite communications, which provide even more distance independence and the potential for storage of large volumes of material in many remote locations so inexpensively that the very existence of a central store of data can be open to doubt. The rise of good, inexpensive, rapid long-distance electronic document storage transmission may change the organizational patterns of individual libraries.[6]

College libraries, like other libraries, must be flexible in order to meet the challenges of an environment made uncertain by the new technology. The traditional bifurcated or trifurcated college library structure described above is undergoing careful scrutiny based on the impact of automation, the implications of other technological developments, and increased understanding of how organizations function.[7] Although the functional departmental structure still prevails, it is not unusual to find a systems development or an operations unit either within a technical services department or as an independent group. Gradually, these units may serve as intralibrary centralizing forces given their potential to encompass cataloging, circulation, and acquisitions.

Automation leads to other organizational changes in libraries. Personnel are added in one unit and eliminated in another. The ratio of professional to support staff tends to shift in favor of the latter as day-to-day operations become more routine—tasks of sorting, filing, counting are taken over by computer. However, new nonprofessional jobs often require increased support staff who have greater skills, experience, and training. Automation may deprofessionalize some formerly professional tasks. For instance, many college libraries are forming production-oriented, rapid cataloging units where the tasks are basically clerical, in contrast to traditional cataloging departments, where the work is primarily of an intellectual nature. There is some evidence of a gradual shift in personnel resources away from cataloging and acquisitions toward public service activities such as reference, library instruction, and aspects of collection development.[8] The impact of technology on the organization of a reference department may be just the opposite. The use of online reference services may necessitate not only additional staff, but service delivered through formal appointments. New databases often require a knowledge of the subjects they cover or, at a minimum, their protocols. Not all members of a reference department can perform all searches.

There may also be a change in the decision-making structure of the library.

> The effect of changes now must be taken into account to a larger degree than before automation. Decisions have become more complex and involve greater risk. Organizational decisions that previously were reached at the departmental level, increasingly have become the responsibility of the top administrative level of the library. As a result, the planning process is more important, with each decision requiring thorough preparation and deliberation.[9]

For college libraries this often means the establishment of coordinating committees or task forces that cross departmental lines. These may be standard or ad hoc groups, depending on the nature of the problem at hand.

A recent trend toward combining academic computing centers and libraries into "Scholarly Information Centers" has met with mixed reactions. Those who oppose this union see differences between the library's and the computing center's use of computers as a major stumbling block. The library, they contend, generally provides access to externally generated information, while computer centers are concerned primarily with internally produced data such as records and intracampus networks. Those who support such a merger see the "Scholarly Information Center" composed of two groups: public or user services, and technical services. Public services would teach patrons to gain access to information (in print or machine-readable form). Technical services would provide support by preparing data for input and making decisions regarding appropriate purchases of systems, documents, hardware, software, and other media.[10]

Although most college libraries are formally organized in a bureaucratic, hierarchical fashion, egalitarian collaboration among departments and a well-developed system of partial participative management exists in most, nonetheless. Teamwork and individual initiative are widely encouraged even in those libraries not following a collegial model of organization. Dickinson College's (Pennsylvania) library is one of the few college libraries organized on a departmental model. As a department of the college it has an elected chair drawn from the ranks of the six professional librarians. The term of office for the chair is three years, and he or she may serve for two terms if re-elected. Only the professional staff operate collegially. Nonlibrary professionals and support staff remain in a bureaucratic structure.[11] A number of problems are associated with the collegial model described above, among which are accountability, organizational flexibility, and the fact that decision making is very time consuming. In addition, communication between collegial and hierarchical structures can be difficult. And finally, many librarians are uninterested in management and are unwilling, and sometimes unable, to serve as chairs.[12]

SUMMARY

In a college library, the primary aim of the administrative structure is to provide the best possible service to library users. A second aim is to ensure efficient and effective operation of the library. Internally, libraries should be arranged with units that perform related tasks placed in close proximity to one another so that work can progress serially. All college libraries, no matter how small, have structures and procedures that can be described graphically in organizational and flow charts.

On the other hand, even small college libraries are in danger of rigid compartmentalization when department members forget to relate the goals of their departments to the mission of the library, or forget they are part of a whole team rather than exclusively catalogers or reference librarians.

The formal organization of a college library, though important, is secondary to the attitudes and behaviors of the administrator and staff. How employees work with one another, the degree to which they understand and share goals, the extent to which the library director and staff can articulate the organizations goals and mount a plan for their achievement, how well the library director can assure the personal well-being and development of its staff—these are of far greater importance to the achievement of the organization.

NOTES

1. Richard R. Hall, *Organizations: Structure and Process* (Englewood Cliffs, N.J.: Prentice-Hall, 1972), 14.

2. Guy Beneveniste, *Mastering the Politics of Planning* (San Francisco: Jossey-Bass, 1989); Robert G. Cope, *Opportunities from Strength: Strategic Planning Clarified with Case Examples*, ASHE-ERIC Higher Education Report #5 (Washington, D.C.: Association for the Study of Higher Education, 1987).

3. Larry Hardesty et al., *Mission Statements for College Libraries*, Clip Note #5 (Chicago: ACRL, 1985), 115.

4. E. A. Wight, "Research in Organization and Administration," *Library Trends* (October 1957): 141-46.

5. Gerard McCabe, "New Patterns for Managing the Small Staff," in *The Smaller Academic Library,* ed. Gerard McCabe (Westport, Conn.: Greenwood Press, 1988), 95.

6. Hugh C. Atkinson, "The Impact of New Technology on Library Organization," *Bowker Annual of Library and Book Trade Information,*. 29th edition (New York: Bowker, 1984), 34.

7. Judy Reynolds and Jo Bell Whitlatch, "Academic Library Services: The Literature of Innovation," *College and Research Libraries* 46 (September 1985): 402-17; Peggy Johnson, "Matrix Management: An Organizational Alternative for Libraries," *Journal of Academic Librarianship* 16 (September 1990): 222-29.

8. Charles Martell, *The Client Centered Academic Library* (Westport, Conn.: Greenwood Press, 1988), 5.

9. Gary Kraske, *The Impact of Automation on the Staff and Organization of a Medium-Sized Academic Library*. ERIC Document 190 153, 12.

10. Diane Cimbala, "The Scholarly Information Center: An Organizational Model," *College and Research Libraries* 48 (August 1987): 394.

11. Joan Bechtel, "Collegial Management Breeds Success," *American Libraries* 12 (November 1981): 605-7.

12. Nancy Brown, "Managing the Coexistence of Hierarchical and Collegial Governance Structures," *College and Research Libraries* 46 (November1985): 478.

Chapter 7

USER SERVICES

Librarians add value to the world's array of information resources. They offer services that focus on the information needs of faculty, students, administrators, and other members of the community by collecting, organizing, and interpreting material that is relevant to the research, teaching, and learning activities of members of the college. Sensitivity to the needs of individual users is a hallmark of quality in college librarianship, and attention to the curriculum is essential to the development of the library's program.

COLLECTION DEVELOPMENT

A rational, well-conceived, systematic program of collection development, management, and acquisition is among the crucial ingredients of a first-rate library. Information is the core around which sound teaching and learning take place in a college, and the library is where access to information is gained. In systems terms, it is the collection, or knowledge base, that is utilized in the process of transforming input to output and outcome. Success or effectiveness of the transformation is influenced by the collection's strengths and weaknesses. The term *collection development*—one aspect of collection management—encompasses a wide range of activities, which, taken together, ensure that a library owns or has provided for regular means of access to the books, periodicals, and other materials required to support the programs of its college. Additional functions involved in collection management include acquisition of materials or electronic services; maintenance and preservation of the collection; and housing, storage, deselecting, and discarding—all within the framework of a policy. A complicated process at best, these tasks involve the efforts of staff, faculty, students, administrators, and representatives of commercial vendors or jobbers.

College library materials collections differ from those in university libraries in a number of important ways. Perhaps the most significant of these is the premium placed by undergraduate institutions on selectivity and by universities on comprehensiveness. Even with the new emphasis among university libraries on cooperation in collection development, the number of titles they hold is still considered the essential figure. On the other hand, while sometimes honored more in the breach, the need for and relevance of each individual title is what should govern decisions about collections in college libraries. Attention to collection maintenance activities, including weeding and conservation also center on the development of useful and appropriate collections more often than preservation of large categories of material.

College library collections are composed of materials for a number of different audiences—with students and faculty as primary recipients and members of the entire academic community in which the college is housed as secondary users. Broadly, these materials can be classified into five major types that are found in every college library.

1. A basic collection for students' curricular needs.
2. Materials to meet faculty research needs.
3. A collection of materials of use to administrators in their work.
4. A good reference collection to help identify materials in the library and resources elsewhere.
5. A collection of cultural and recreational materials.

The curriculum, faculty interests, and size of the acquisitions budget are important factors bearing on the materials collection development policy in the college library. Academic libraries spend, on average, 37 percent of their budgets on acquisitions.[1] Increasing amounts of acquisitions funds may be used to provide access to material, but the majority of funds are allocated for the purchase of materials. Limited financial resources for collection development necessitate difficult choices on how funds are allocated. To some extent, it can be considered a zero-sum exercise. The selection of any major expensive set for instance, may mean the rejection of other needed works or the postponement of their purchase.

A recurring challenge of college librarianship is to allocate the materials budget among competing subject claims equitably.

Unfortunately, there is no single agreed-upon method for apportioning funds. Each institution must develop its own approach and guidelines.

In colleges where faculty retain primary responsibility for the materials collection, there is often a fixed allocation of the book budget, although many librarians consider the allocation suggestive rather than constraining. When librarians make the bulk of the selection decisions, there may or may not be a formally allocated budget. Even in the absence of specific dollar allocations, however, librarians, by virtue of their decisions establish distribution patterns. Allocations are generally made in two ways, usually a combination of both:

1. By format (books, periodicals, microforms, etc.). The median allocation among liberal arts college libraries for periodicals alone, exclusive of binding, is 42 percent of the materials budget.[2]
2. By substantive area (scholarly discipline).

It is likely that, in the foreseeable future, format will be a less salient consideration than content in the allocation of materials budgets. Science information, for instance, is currently found most often in periodicals and increasingly in electronic form. Literature, on the other hand, still appears as print on paper in a bound volume.

Responsibility for allocating the materials budget generally rests with librarians, although the advice of the library committee or other faculty and administrators is often sought for both practical and political reasons.

Many colleges now use allocation formulas to distribute their acquisitions budget. These schemes have evolved from simple to sophisticated. The major attraction of the budgeting formula is "rhetorical in that it serves to convince faculty members and departments that their allocations are fair."[3] On the other hand, critics of formula allocations contend that using one provides evidence to skeptical faculty and administrators that librarians have little professional expertise to offer and are willing to trust collection development to generic formulas rather than their own knowledge.

It is important that librarians each year request sufficient funding for needed materials, utilizing, if possible, comparable data from peer institutions, standards, publishing industry sources, and recent college history. Caution is advised when using these data to mount arguments for increased funding. Peer comparisons may have a shock effect and ACRL standards can illuminate weaknesses in a collection. Neither, however, substitutes for linking a request for additional funds to institutional priorities and new programs. Faculty must be led to conclude that the library has realistic expectations and is a good provider and manager of currently available resources. Immediate improvements to the materials budget rarely result from such applications, but the argument must continually be made.

Size, Use, and Selectors

College administrators, faculty members, publishers, and politicians often use numbers of volumes—the mere size of a collection—as a benchmark of achievement. Librarians are not exempt from the charms of this popular fallacy. Yet, as every sensible person knows, the value of a college library is determined by its quality, not its size. Everyone agrees that libraries should be "good," but affixing criteria to "goodness" is almost impossible.

Library use studies have consistently demonstrated that only a small part of most collections find their way into the hands of users. Trueswell concluded that 80 percent of the circulation is satisfied by 20 percent of the stocked items and that 99 percent of the circulation demand is satisfied by 60 percent of a collection.[4] Larry Hardesty found that 80 percent of need was satisfied by 30 percent of the collection.[5]

Recent studies about the use of academic libraries indicate that:

1. Overall use is lower than we think, or like to think.
2. In-house use and external circulation are correlated.
3. Use is highly concentrated over a small number of titles, and previous use is generally the best single predictor of subsequent use.
4. Interest in materials is subject to a process (generally asymptotic) of obsolescence.
5. Foreign language materials are significantly underutilized in proportion to holdings.[6]

Despite the new emphasis on access rather than acquisition, libraries will be responsible for providing locally the materials required to meet the routine needs of their users. College libraries will continue to devote a large portion of their resources to their own collection development because each institution will remain the primary source of material to meet undergraduate requirements. Such development should be coupled with ongoing evaluation of different areas of the collection. There is always a need for periodic weeding of outdated material, attention to the preservation needs of a select group of items, integration of gifts into the collection, and maintenance of the periodicals collection. Whether local access is in electronic or print formats, the issues of accessibility, integrity, and usefulness of the material for the needs of undergraduates remain more important than any goal of comprehensiveness.

Historically, there has been a persistent and largely unchallenged tenet of college library acquisitions policy that teaching faculty would have the dominant voice in the materials selection process. A number of college librarians feel that the time for reconsideration of this policy is long overdue. Good reasons exist for faculty making the bulk of the selections; good reasons abound for librarians to play the same role. The following is a summary of arguments for assigning faculty primary responsibility in selecting library materials. Teaching faculty know the literature of their own subject fields best; they can identify what material they need for research; and they are best prepared to select course-related material. Among the arguments mounted against faculty doing the bulk of selection are that they are often uninterested, and tend to be narrow in their selections, often stressing advanced work in their own subject fields and forgetting that the mission of the library is to support undergraduate instruction, not research. In addition, they may be unfamiliar with current materials in their fields. Further, faculty do not recognize gaps and weaknesses in the collection as a whole, nor can they observe, as do librarians, what is being used. A real danger exists that gaps will develop when there is no department for a particular subject or if interdisciplinary materials fall into the chasm between them. Finally, an allocation controlled by a department lessens flexibility and the ability to make midcourse corrections as a control against over- and underspending.

Who chooses better materials for the library, faculty or library staff? Better, in this context as in so many others relating to libraries, has been defined as amount of "use" of library materials. Research into the question has produced ambiguous or contradictory data. Evans found that titles selected by librarians circulate more frequently than those chosen by faculty or book jobbers. Bingham replicated Evans's study and found books selected by faculty circulated more frequently than those selected by librarians, except in humanities. Geyer studied community colleges and found no difference.[7]

Collection Development Policy

Most librarians agree, in principle at least, that a collection development policy is essential. It should include as considerations the college's curriculum, its goals, attention to the quality of documents, level of material to be collected, use of library materials, and meeting faculty research interests. Along with the collection development statement, the collection management policy should include a retention, discard, and weeding policy, and a preservation policy that includes binding, microformating, restoration, housing, storage, and housekeeping. A collection development and management policy includes, in one form or another, the following elements:

1. *Overview.* The collection management policy is framed by the scope, objectives, and goals of the library, as is any policy. These are to be clearly articulated at the outset. Preliminary material also describes the community; identifies clientele; states the parameters of the collection; describes in detail the types of programs or patron needs that are to be met by the collection; includes a section of general limitations and priorities that determine how the collection will be developed; and discusses in detail the library's participation in cooperative collection development programs.

2. *Scope of Collection.* This describes in detail the subject areas and formats collected. The policy should set out priorities and levels of collecting intensity.

3. *Collection Responsibility.* There should be a clear statement about who is responsible for selection and for deselecting, and what guidelines are to be used in the process.

4. *Miscellaneous Issues.* These include: gifts, weeding and discarding; the bases for decisions regarding binding, housing, equipment, microfilming, and preservation, restoration, or replacement; and how to handle complaints.

5. *Intellectual Freedom.* A statement committing the library to support of academic and intellectual freedom and to prohibit censorship should appear in every library collection development policy.

At the heart of the college, libraries are sustained and nourished by their collections. For librarians, collections represent their enduring legacy to the institution. For faculty, the collections may be *the* reason for the library.

CATALOGING AND CLASSIFICATION

For all books, journals, and most other types of material added to the library, catalogs provide access to the materials by supplying brief descriptions of them. This process is known as cataloging. Staff also determine where each new addition belongs in the library's scheme of book arrangement. This is called classification. In some library schools, the term *organization of knowledge* is used to encompass both traditional cataloging and classification activities and newer forms of indexing, document tagging, and hypertext linkage creation for books, articles, files and other sources of data of interest to libraries. Regardless of the term, agreement remains that there is a need to establish principles and techniques for assisting users with searches, principles that distinguish among items and feature categories related to ways in which humans search for answers to both formulated and unformulated questions. The past three decades have witnessed a revolution in cataloging methods caused primarily by five interrelated developments.

1. *The creation of a standard format for entering cataloging data into a computer.* The cataloging standard that was developed in the late 1960s at the Library of Congress under the leadership of Henriette Avram became known as the MARC (Machine-Readable Cataloging) format. MARC established a standard format for entering and storing descriptive cataloging information into the computer.

2. *The adoption of a new cataloging code.* AACR II (*AngloAmerican Cataloging Rules*, 2nd edition) Revised is the authority for descriptive cataloging. It specifies the form of entry a cataloger will use to establish the bibliographic record for an item, based on the item itself. AACR II replaced AACR I in 1978, but it was not implemented nationally until 1981.

3. *The development of cataloging in publication.* The Cataloging in Publication program (CIP) was begun in 1971 and now includes more than 2,500 publishers who

submit books in galley form or provide prepublication data to the Library of Congress, where catalogers determine the classification number and catalog entries. When the book is published, the information appears on the verso of the title page.

4. *The cooperative development of telecommunications based bibliographic utilities.* Networks such as OCLC, RLIN, and WLN are formed by the agreement of member libraries to use a centralized computer system linked through telecommunications lines to terminals at the local sites.

5. *The availability of personal computers and local area networks.* The creation of local and remote online public access catalogs of library holdings are one result; full text database development is another. Each library makes the change as soon as funding permits. Benefits include being able to search by keyword as well as Library of Congress subject headings and access to other library collections, reference materials, and the resources of the Internet.

The work of cataloging and classifying the typical collection of English language material has been greatly simplified by the existence of cataloging records for most of the material purchased since 1977. If the exact record is not available, there is usually a record that is a close variant or one that can serve as a model. Older materials, more specialized materials, and items in foreign languages are often also available, and the need for doing original cataloging is greatly reduced.

To some, it appears that the cataloging challenges of the immediate future, except in the largest research libraries with special collections, are in the realm of designing graphic user interfaces, or Web sites, for homepage texts that feature Internet access solutions. Others recognize that the tasks of listing and maintaining a local database with several hundred thousand items is also a challenge for libraries. Catalogers have always done authority work—establishing names, series, uniform titles, and subject headings. But with online systems, meticulous authority work is fast replacing other tasks as the number-one priority. Good authority-control work assures that only correct records are retrieved. For this reason, authority work has moved from its position of near invisibility a decade ago to one recognized as a major cataloging concern at the national level.[8] One catalog librarian describes his work as a database editor; another sees herself as a problem solver concerned with establishing and maintaining the integrity of the library's official records of its holdings The aim is integrity; users should be able to trust that the catalog accurately reflects the holdings and services of the library.

Recent research about user behavior at catalogs suggests the experience is difficult in both card and electronic catalogs. Users do not distinguish between author entries and author as subject. Nor do they recognize a catalog's limitations—for instance that the catalog only contains monograph holdings from a certain date. User education is always needed.

REFERENCE SERVICE

The success of a reference transaction for a college librarian is defined as having provided not only a good answer—one that responds adequately to a stated need—but one that has successfully transferred the skills both to acquire an immediate answer and to locate information in the future. Instruction in how to gain access to various types of library resources is often linked to particular information retrieval problems.

Technological developments have provided reference librarians with powerful new information locators, among them online bibliographic databases, CD-ROM products, and the Internet. While these new approaches offer information-retrieval capabilities unheard of a decade ago, they also present substantial challenges in developing the skills associated with their use to today's college users. If libraries do not play a leading role in providing access to the new information services, then a part of the libraries' purpose will be abnegated and they may have trouble defining their function or demonstrating their worth.

One of the challenges and responsibilities of being a college reference librarian is to ensure that first meetings with new students are pleasant and significant, occur fairly soon after the student arrives on campus, and do not represent final encounters. A distinction between public and college reference work is the extent to which teaching users how to acquire information is part of the process of answering questions. While college students may occasionally seek specific and definitive information, more often their quest is for more general subject material. College reference librarians draw on different skills than do public librarians to aid students in the solution of their problems. In general, it is the duty of the academic reference librarian to help students learn how to find the material themselves, to develop their own information-seeking and interpretation skills.

The past decade has been characterized by increasing attention to precision in information retrieval; to looking at the relevance and pertinence of answers; to examining the role of intermediaries in the search process; to defining problem statements; and to insuring the appropriateness of the reference interview. Reference librarians help students hone in on topics and narrow the parameters of their searches; it is a consultative process shaped by ambiguities in human communication as well as by complicated negotiations. In Karen Markey's words, "Question negotiation is an illustration of a complicated interaction between two individuals in which one person tries to describe for another nothing he knows, but rather something he does not know."[9] Question negotiation may be centered around the review of citations. As citations spew from electronic sources, distinguishing among them and identifying those with the greatest potential to be of use challenges students at terminals, the reference librarian working with them, and the staff in interlibrary loan. Each has a reason for wanting a successful completion of the search, and each will benefit from the student mastering the process of information analysis.

Too often, professional reference librarians in colleges spend time doing clerical work, providing simple directional answers to questions, or helping patrons to learn whether the library owns a specific known item. It has been the custom to staff reference desks with only trained librarians. Today, some libraries are modifying that tradition at least to the extent of experimenting with the use of upperclass students and support staff with reference department training to serve alongside librarians. Other libraries also schedule support staff to work independently for the hours known to be less hectic and use students to supplement service during busy hours. These modifications may enable reference librarians to offer service to individuals on a regular basis and focus attention on a full program of reference services, including development of the reference collection, creation of bibliographies and guides in print and electronic form, provision of a program of bibliographic instruction, and working with faculty on behalf of the students and for faculty research needs.

At times, program adjustments are necessary in the face of shrinking budgets. On such occasions the question of charging for services arises. As further advances in technologies become available, new dilemmas continue to surface concerning who should pay for them, who might benefit, and whether they should be implemented. American librarians generally agree that access to information in a barrier-free manner is an important occupational value and that any inhibiting factor is to be viewed negatively.[10] They hesitate to charge users. Some do so only when there is either no other way to introduce a service deemed important or when the class of users is considered capable of paying and is not the primary audience. Others reject entirely the notion of payment for library use, arguing that when fees are levied for online searches, the result is to discriminate in favor of the "haves" as opposed to the "have-nots".

When we have access to electronic texts, will we have to pay for every use of an item, including browsing? Who owns information? The now popular conception of information as a commodity is currently being challenged, based, in part, on the argument that a great deal of information is generated from taxpayer-funded government reports. Librarians and producers of information may view these issues differently. Academic librarians cannot expect to develop or receive significant new services without the profession reaching agreement with the publishing industry on the general rights and responsibilities of each party. The issue of charging fees is one that continues to test the values we have traditionally shared as librarians.

EDUCATING THE LIBRARY USER

Among the newly embraced basic objectives for a college education is to prepare students for lifelong learning; that is, to equip them with the skills and tools to become informed about the matters that will have importance in their lives. The knowledge explosion of the last two decades has served to convince educators that understanding process is as important as studying practice and that students must learn not only bodies of information, but also how to learn. In the so-called information society, attention is focused on how people acquire information and how they turn it to knowledge once it has been acquired.

To that end, librarians must first define the role their instruction programs are to play, always within the context of their parent institution. This entails careful planning, setting objectives, and evaluation. Second, the instructional role must be interpreted to funding sources, administrators, faculty, and students. And finally, librarians must gain widespread acceptance of the role. Although there is common agreement, based on research findings, that most students lack the basic skills and knowledge to use the library effectively, some college libraries may choose to target certain groups as the first to receive instruction. For instance:

1. Academically less prepared students may warrant special consideration as a result of poor educational preparation, access to English only as a second language, or lack of motivation.
2. Student library workers, particularly if the library is one which chooses to have desks serviced by students, may rank high on the priority list.
3. Faculty. Good reasons abound for targeting faculty for library instruction. Some librarians contend that the most successful student library instruction comes through faculty who have received intensive orientation and instruction from the library staff. In any case faculty are crucial to the success of any user-education program.[11]

Faculty intransigence is often blamed for lack of success of library instruction proposals and programs. Yet, librarians must bear some of the blame, particularly for their inattentiveness to the importance of explaining the goals of library instruction to their constituents. For instance, faculty often understand student research needs quite differently than do librarians. They do not realize that the research training in library skills they have experienced as graduate students does not, nor should it, resemble the kind of research students will undertake at the undergraduate level.[12]

Ways should be sought to provide incentives to energize faculty to incorporate appropriate library instruction modules in their courses. When any area of the college develops or sponsors workshops devoted to new methods of teaching or learning, there are opportunities to promote library instruction. The sponsor may not realize this at first, and librarians may need to seek permission to attend. Workshops that focus on courses in the process of being changed to incorporate new scholarship, the development of a new course by a faculty member, and new initiatives to improve learning are all good opportunities to reach faculty. Another strategy is to inform faculty—delicately—of student difficulties in using the library to write papers. Documenting the results of a user-education program, comparing, for instance, the performance of students who receive library instruction with those who do not can have a positive effect on faculty attitudes about library instruction. After all, as Patricia Breivik has said, "Politics not only concerns what a library does but what people know about what it is doing. Being too busy doing library instruction to evaluate it in terms meaningful to faculty, administrators, board members, and legislators is tantamount to committing suicide in these days of tightening funds for education." [13]

There are as many opinions about what should be included in user instruction as there are user instruction librarians. In its initial stages, the thrust of bibliographic instruction is best approached as problem solving. Students learn how to ask a question, how to determine whether it is answerable, how to discover whether it has been asked before, and how it may differ from similar ones that have been posed. Second, students are shown how to approach information. This might include an understanding of the research process, research strategy, and knowledge of tools and resources. Third, students are taught about the nature of evidence—how to evaluate it, how to assess what is enough, and how to determine the validity of a statement. A final component should consider documentation and the use of citations. The importance of contradictions, individual perceptions, points of view, and analysis should be introduced when students seem ready to handle ambiguity. At this point, the library should be treated as evidence to be examined.[14]

At a more advanced level, user instruction is discipline oriented. Students gain an awareness of information resources in their fields, as well as the structure of literature in that subject and its research patterns and strategies. In addition, attention is given to evaluation of sources in light of the behavioral patterns in the discipline.

The structures of library instruction most commonly practiced in academic libraries are course-related instruction, course integrated instruction, team teaching, separate credit courses, and library workshops.

The structure selected depends as much on faculty attitudes and preferences as it does on the library staff. Faculty provide the greatest impetus for student use of the library and for the program of library instruction.

Perhaps the most frequently chosen structure is course-related. Individual professors set aside time, usually a single class period, during which librarians lecture in a classroom or give a tour while describing and displaying specific—usually subject-related—reference materials. In this situation, instruction librarians are challenged to present, in no more than fifty minutes, everything they think students might need to know to successfully retrieve information in the subject area.

This is particularly difficult if the instruction is attached to first-year seminars, basic writing courses, or other general-education requirements. Too often, library skills are taught in a vacuum, without reference to their application. A good learning experience is need-driven and active. Without a research project, what is learned may be irrelevant and/or quickly forgotten. Other approaches include library instruction integrated into a research methods course, separate library instruction courses, and mainstreaming of library instructional materials into all courses (perhaps by the development of assignments focusing on research-strategy skills) and term-paper counseling sessions offered by the reference department to groups and to individuals who come to the reference counter. What is important to remember is that with library-use instruction, as with other skills, one-shot training is never enough. A good program includes sequentially planned instruction, progresses with the curriculum and is based on the student's cognitive abilities and levels. A great program has all of the above and is recognized as such by faculty and administration as an important part of the student's collegiate experience.

CIRCULATION

The final step in the process of making library materials available, once they have been acquired, cataloged, and identified as needed by a user, is circulation. No matter how a given library determines what it will borrow and what it will buy, getting the desired book, article, facsimile document, or electronic text into the hands of the reader calls for the development of circulation policies and procedures. These decisions are based on answers to the following policy questions:

1. Who can borrow library materials?
2. What materials will be lent?
3   For how long may they be borrowed?
4. What will happen if they are not returned?
5. Who may have remote access to the system?
6. Which materials will be placed on reserve?
7. Will interlibrary loans be restricted?
8. What, if any, services will have charges?

Each academic library makes its own case for its particular mix of on-site materials and off-site access options.[15] The availability of technology, the amount of space, the strength of a materials budget, the location, the expectations of faculty and students, the availability of resources and services in cost-effective alternative electronic formats, and the wishes of the administration and the library faculty and staff are some of the variables surrounding the choices made. Michael Buckland's reminder that a book at hand is used more than a book on the other side of the campus, let alone on another campus or in another state, is not to be dismissed.[16]

The practice of putting items that are required reading by faculty on reserve began to flourish when faculty moved away from primary reliance on textbooks. Students who use the collection find it a quick and reliable way to fulfill requirements; staff who service the area find it labor intensive and subject to review with respect to adherence to copyright provisions. Experiments with electronic versions are in embryonic stages. More prevalent are alternatives to reserves such as the sale of faculty generated, commercially produced packets of course-related readings in the campus bookstore. If the course reserve service moves from the library completely, there will be a corresponding loss in the ability of the library staff to interact with faculty and students and to have their fingers on the pulse of the curriculum.

Interlibrary loan may be handled in circulation, in reference, or in its own department. Even in libraries with little automation, interlibrary loan activity has increased significantly in the decades since the emergence of OCLC. Sources are easier to find, and the ease of finding encourages libraries to borrow more freely from other libraries. Borrowing becomes a substitute for ownership when a library decides to rely on acquiring material as it is requested rather than in advance. This is becoming known as the just-in-time versus just-in-case scenario. As the philosophy of just-in-time access has grown and the practice of just-in-case collection development has declined a variety of document delivery services have begun to emerge. Some are built upon altruistic interlibrary loan practices, and use reciprocal borrowing arrangements and facsimile machines to offer rapid response times; others rely on commercial services and may require some libraries to impose fees for service.

The availability of indexing services on the Internet gives libraries the ability to offer users a table of contents for journals and an article delivery service linked to the library's online public access catalog. These services, and others like them, narrow the boundaries between the physical site of a given library and the expanse of library services available through the virtual library.[17] Eventually, where the boundaries are may matter less than where the opportunities for creative library service flourish.

TECHNOLOGY SERVICES

The provision and servicing of microform and microfiche collections, microformat readers, and reader printers has been problematic to academic libraries for over fifty years. Patrons find the format less than desirable to use but are willing to utilize it when the machines are reliable and the print quality of any copy is good. Library staff struggle to provide sufficient maintenance to cover heavy use and fund replacement and upgrading of equipment as needed. Decisions about which parts of a collection are suitable for microformat are also contentious. Scholars want to see original documents, students want the hard copy of the current journal, and librarians want to ensure preservation of source material and availability of back issues of journals. Each group will accept and tolerate the necessity for the microfilm or microfiche format. No group, except perhaps conservationists, truly embraces micrographic sources as its first choice.

Library experience with photocopy services is happier to relate. Patrons welcome the technology and accept the responsibility of paying for it on a per-use basis. Library staffs find that use of this technology enhances their ability to offer good service in reserves and interlibrary loan, and experience a positive correlation between the presence of photocopy machines and a reduction in the mutilation of collections, especially journal issues. However, there are problems related to adherence to the fair use provisions of the copyright laws. Fair use requires that libraries seek permission from the holders of copyrights when there is a need to make multiple copies of a given work; fair use also means that libraries perform an educational role in this area with respect to helping faculty prepare materials to be placed on course reserves and in informing users of public photocopy machines about the law. What will constitute fair use in the electronic era remains undefined. But some provision for access and replication of material for individual scholarly and teaching purposes without permission and payment for each action is essential, and the principle must be supported vigorously by academic librarians interested in protecting the growth of scholarship.

Each of these technologies has its primary effect at the local level of library service, although the use of photocopying in interlibrary loan departments increases the interaction among libraries, and there has been some intralibrary collaboration to develop certain microform collections. With the introduction of technologies based on the use of mainframe computers and a national standard for cataloging (the Library of Congress MARC record), the traditional walls between libraries began to crumble. OCLC began in the 1970s, and its success, along with the success of other national bibliographic utilities, has led to significant changes in the provision of library services. One library can now copy some of its cataloging from another library and also share its own original cataloging records. The availability of the OCLC database for interlibrary loan has meant exponential growth in interlibrary loan activity. The development of turnkey software for public access catalogs and the ever-increasing power of personal computers results in ever-decreasing development cycles. Parallel to this effort is the work related to the development of CD-ROM hardware and software, a technology that offers academic libraries opportunities to provide enriched indexing services, delivery of full text and access to catalog information for groups of libraries. In the early and mid-1980s, the goal of many libraries was to select, acquire, and install an automated library system. Those in institutions with sufficient resources achieved the goal earlier and moved on to explore other technology-related goals. Some academic institutions are still seeking funding for a full online public access system for their campus, and rely on partial access through consortia funded by federal and state grants designed to foster library cooperation for the good of all citizens.

Beginning in the late 1980s, a technology goal in many libraries has been to strengthen the campus technological infrastructure by wiring the entire campus to provide faster data transmission with sufficient power for good graphic displays. The cost of being up-to-date is considerable and calls for collaborative efforts between libraries, computing centers, and central administration. Faculty interest, sound budgeting and intelligent visions about a network's potential are three components of successful applications. Computer center personnel want the power of high-speed computing available in classrooms and offices; librarians want students and faculty to have access to the library's catalog and collection of CD-ROMs; and more and more all groups want access to data available on the Internet, a government-sponsored system of linking high-speed computers to facilitate sharing of data. As campuses are wired, information sources available through the Internet are highlighted on local systems' home page menus. Service centers in libraries and computer centers have begun to explore different organizational structures to reflect the changed technological environment of distributed access.

Discussion has centered on training users to master the new technologies, with some attention also given to the implications of electronic access for provision of services at a distance. In the early 1990s, large numbers of library catalogs and some text-based collections became available on the Internet. The presence of the collections has led to much discussion about the emergence of the virtual library, or library without walls. This is an ongoing concern that includes some soul searching about the role of the physical library in the future. The rapid acceptance of software designed to make use of the Internet easier for the general public is accelerating the discussion as each library and library user finds that some subject control or filter is needed to avoid the problem of information deluge. For some libraries, the response is to highlight their ability to shape resource pathfinders through the creation of home pages on the World Wide Web. For others, the appropriate response is to link to other libraries' home pages, and reaffirm the wisdom of supporting a carefully selected collection and a strong reference and library instruction program. Each library is painfully aware that the rate of change has accelerated and necessitates constant upgrading of technological skills for staff members.

INTERPRETATION AND OUTREACH

The functions of the college library are often not fully understood by those who are responsible for its welfare at the top level or by those who use its services. Even less well understood are the activities performed by staff. Students often think a librarian is there to "check out books." The goal of interpretation is to communicate to each potential library user or user group those features of the library's program most pertinent to their interest.

Many library directors think about how best to promote their services, and some even allocate funds for that purpose. Fewer, however, understand the importance to library interpretation of their public presence, or that of their staff, on the campus. Consciously or unconsciously, everyone connected with the library performs an interpretation function. Any carefully conceived interpretation program includes both personal contact between librarians and those with whom they must interact, and a program of planned distribution of written information about the library. The persons to whom the library must interpret its work are: (1) campus personnel, including college administrative officers, boards, committees, faculty, and students; and (2) off-campus groups such as the local community, alumni, Friends of the Library, and professional associations. Written information about the library is disseminated principally through annual reports, handbooks, college catalogs, local student and library newspapers, articles in college or professional periodicals, booklists, bulletin boards, signs, and exhibits. The creation of material for a college-wide information system in the World Wide Web environment offers libraries the potential to bridge the worlds of campus and off-campus communication systems and accelerate the process of receiving feedback on their services.

Library directors who participate in campus-wide planning and development efforts have opportunities to tie the needs of the library to other campus projects, or at least to alert others to library needs. Whether and the extent to which librarians participate in faculty meetings varies on each campus and controls the degree to which faculty meetings represent a fitting place to discuss library concerns or promote library-sponsored events. Major changes in library policy are best presented in person to the faculty, but only after they have been shared with the relevant committees or individual faculty members and assurances have been received that these groups or individuals are prepared to publicly support proposed changes.

Most librarians find it necessary to communicate in writing with faculty once or twice a year. Their memoranda or newsletters may contain explanations of new bibliographic instruction opportunities or new database searching services, or other programs too important to relegate to the grapevine or chance visits by the faculty to the library. Whereas the director bears chief responsibility for maintaining good working relations with the president, senior administrators, and the faculty as a body, members of the library staff, including student assistants, *are* the library to students and must bear a substantial amount of responsibility for impressions this group has of the library.

Students meet the library as they would a person. Clearly, staff must welcome them warmly and with an attitude that conveys helpfulness and interest. There can be no room on a library staff for employees who cannot balance concern for library procedures with a sympathetic understanding of student or faculty behavior, or who have difficulty dealing with people whose backgrounds differ from their own. Conflicts and problems with patrons require delicate handling in order that mutually acceptable solutions may be reached with a minimum of rancor. Library staff know intimately how many errors the library can and does make. In view of this, it seems foolish to adopt a posture that suggests that the library is always right. Even when enforcing rules, staff must guard against permitting a natural concern for order and fairness to deteriorate into rigidity. How libraries view their users is made manifest not only in over-the-counter transactions, but in words and the tone used in written communications such as overdue notices, closed reserve procedures, and instructional signs.

Occasional audits taken to ensure that the reality of daily library service coheres with descriptions of it appearing in promotional material, or with the library administration's understanding of how it is to be delivered, may produce surprising results. Problems emerge. If the same ones appear in the suggestion box, prompt attention is required.

Opinion surveys about the library can also used to learn how users feel about the services they are receiving. Although surveys find users generally satisfied, major problem areas can surface.

Some off-campus groups that use the college library can become important supporters of the library. These include local residents, alumni, donors, and Friends of the Library. An association of library constituents brings together a group of men and women who love books, reading, and libraries, and who are willing to help the college library by publicly proclaiming its virtues and by adding to its resources.

Media commonly used to interpret the library to its community include annual reports, handbooks, college catalogs, student newspapers, newsletters, booklists, exhibits, signs and communication networks. Most libraries will use all of these media at one time or another to describe and interpret themselves. With desktop publishing, libraries now can make every document they generate look as though it had emerged directly from the college print shop.

Libraries have traditionally mounted in-house exhibits. Displays are planned to mesh with campus events—Black History Month or college anniversary—to highlight a particular collection of materials. One exhibit may especially appeal to students, another attract an audience of senior faculty. However, each exhibit, regardless of its subject or particular appeal, can in some way exploit and call attention to library collections.

Other contributions that librarians can make to campus cultural and intellectual life may be more subtle and less apparent. Many college librarians have willingly accepted the challenge of promoting reading on their campuses, working with faculty to encourage attendance at author visits and to develop browsing collections, new book areas, and other mechanisms to encourage reading and cultural development. Visual literacy is also worthy of support, and film is a medium that attracts most college students.

The outside world is often unfamiliar with what the college library is and what it would like to be. A rigorous program of interpretation will help to inform constituents about its programs, services, and resources.

SUMMARY

With the rapid introduction of electronic alternatives to traditional library sources and services, librarians face the challenge of delivering appropriate services to users. Designing filters to help users find appropriate information becomes as important as amassing information sources. The filter may be a staff member who assists a user puzzled about the citations he sees on the screen; the filter may be judicious selection of sources to mount locally; the filter may be the home page created to guide Internet use. Each staff action in information services design and delivery should add value to a previously undifferentiated mass of information by adding the qualities of order, evaluation ,and interpretation to the data at hand. As the power of computers is tapped for information-management work, distinctions between and among the traditional tasks of cataloging, reference, acquisitions and circulation staff blur, merge, and evolve into new and shared public service challenges, often challenges shared with the staff of the academic computer center on campus.

NOTES

1. Richard Hume Werking, "Collection Growth and Expenditures," *College and Research Libraries* 52 (January 1991): 15.

2. Data concerning serial expenditures as a percentage of materials expenditures for a group of sixty-two liberal arts college libraries, in authors' possession.

3. Jasper Shad as quoted in Ross Atkinson, "Old Forms: New Forms: The Challenge of Collection Development," *College and Research Libraries* 50 (January 1989): 512.

4. Richard Trueswell, "Some Behavioral Patterns of Library Users: The 80/20 Rule," *Wilson Library Bulletin* 43 (January 1969): 458-61.

5. Richard Johnson, "The College Library Collection," in *Advances in Librarianship*, vol. 14, ed. Wesley Simonton (Chicago: Academic Press, 1986), 148.

6. Paul Metz, *The Landscapes of Literature* (Chicago: American Library Association, 1984), 108.

7. Summarized in Mary Sellen, "Budget Formula Allocations: A Review Essay," *Collection Development* 9 (Winter 1987) : 13-24.

8. Janet Swan Hill, "The Cataloging Half of Cataloging and Classification, 1986," *Library Resources and Technical Services* 31 (October/December 1987): 323.

9. Karen Markey, "Levels of Formulation in Negotiation of Information Need during the Online Research Interview," *Information Processing and Management* 17 (1981): 223.

10. Brian Nielson, "Allocating Costs, Thinking about Values," *Journal of Academic Librarianship* 15 (September 1989): 214.

11. Patricia Senn Breivik, *Planning the Library Instruction Program* (Chicago: American Library Association, 1982), 4.

12. Stephen Stoan, "Research and Library Skills," *College and Research Libraries* 45 (March 1984): 99.

13. Breivik, *Planning,* 11-14.

14. John Cowley and Nancy Hammond, *Educating Information Users in Universities* (London: The British Library, 1987), 22.

15. Barbra Buckner Higginbothan, *Access versus Assets: A Comprehensive Guide to Resource Sharing for Libraries* (Chicago: American Library Association, 1993).

16. Michael Buckland, "Library Materials: Paper, Microform, Database," *College and Research Libraries* 49 (March 1988): 117-118.

17. Karen M. Drabenstott, *Analytical Review of the Library of the Future* (Washington, D.C.: Council on Library Resources, 1994).

Chapter 8

THE LIBRARY STAFF

All employees share responsibility for the articulation and development of a library's vision, service ethos, and humane work environment. The specifics of each person's task may differ, but the work contract each accepts upon employment assumes a productive use of all employees' time.

During her study of the activities and behaviors of academic library directors, Joanne Euster was able to isolate four main types. These she named Energizers, Sustainers, Politicians and Retirees. Energizers, she found are most closely associated with change in libraries. Retirees are content to rest on their laurels. Sustainers and Politicians, respectively, concern themselves primarily with existing processes or with cultivating people.[1] This same typology can be extended to all members of the staff. Good directors and good staffs combine characteristics of energizers, politicians, and sustainers, but even the best librarian knows that it is possible to begin the day as a dedicated energizer and feel like a forced retiree at six o'clock that afternoon. In these situations, a mix of humility, humor, insight, dedication and intelligence can overcome the sometimes harsh realities of trying to effect and affect changes in the intimate environment that characterizes most college communities. What motivates a library director and staff to continue, and keeps the college library in need of their services, is their vision of what constitutes good library service and their steadfast intention to transform that vision into reality on the campus they serve. One person may produce the desired outcome by using political persuasion, another by employing systems theory, and still another by coaching staff.

VALUES AND VISION

Despite ambiguities about the definition of quality in academic libraries, all good directors and library staff members recognize how collection development, technical services, technology, staff development, and public services, including the information literacy program, should obtain under ideal conditions. It is toward this optimum level of service delivery that library directors aspire and channel their energies. Successful directors clearly articulate their visions and provide plans of action to accomplish them in ways that convince other administrators, faculty, and library staff of their rightness and achievability. Visions are always based on a deep understanding of the educational mission of the college. They are supplemented by familiarity with faculty and student strengths, and informed by the need to translate national concerns into local issues. A grasp of the nature and structure of academic disciplines offered by colleges lends depth to visions and enables directors to be active participants in the scholarly life of the community. It is as crucial for librarians to be cognizant of the intellectual arguments of the decade as it is for them to know how people learn or how to retrieve information. The ability to join the discourse leads to acceptance and support of librarians' visions.

Library directors are often called upon to share their ideas with constituents. Library staff also have these opportunities. Sometimes faculty are the audience; other times, their remarks may be directed to trustees, administrators, Friends of the Library groups, current or prospective students, or potential donors. A carefully crafted and well-delivered message articulating options and potentials for the library's future helps to expand the listener's horizons and understanding of change, thereby enhancing the possibilities of realizing the director's and staff's shared vision for the library. At other times the best speech is action, especially if the action of giving good service reinforces the library's vision.

Unfortunately, vision is easy to lose in the course of day-to-day preoccupations and once lost, vision is difficult to recapture as events shift, personnel change, and institutional goals alter. Without vision, directors run the risk of being manipulated into conceding staff positions, portions of the materials budget, or other elements of the program. Without vision, librarians and staff can confuse the daily routine with long-term goals. Each can reinforce their visions by clarifying what is most important for the library, returning to the important texts of the library field, keeping up with the new literature, and, if time allows, engaging in research.

Visions are influenced by context and by the values brought to it. A value orientation is forged in the crucible of personal and professional experience, and guides the way an individual understands the ethical issues that are of importance in our society and applies them to the library. Broadened cultural horizons and a quest for knowledge lead successful librarians to design programs that allow users to undertake research and enjoy knowledge for its own sake. Those with a narrow technical approach and limited imagination find the task more difficult.

Librarians may hold alternate value orientations toward some issues. U.S. librarians, however, should accept and be committed to the precepts of the First Amendment to the U.S. Constitution, the *Library Bill of Rights*, and AAUP's stance on academic freedom. The basic assumptions of these documents serve as litmus tests to govern how controversies involving library materials, staff, policies, and services are resolved.

Librarians thus accept as a tenet of faith the principle that all users must have equality of access and opportunity to use information without regard to differences in race, culture, ethnicity, economic status, education, or sexual preference. They use these principles to develop operational definitions of access in a given situation.

Directors and staff transmit to users the belief that good libraries make a difference, that societies are better because librarians and libraries exist. They demonstrate what it means to provide excellent library service in a pluralistic multicultural society.[2]

LEADERSHIP

Confirming that librarians are planning, instructing, and evaluating work, and not performing clerical tasks, is one of the director's oversight responsibilities. Simultaneously, assuring that support staff, including student staff, have opportunities to experience some of the real rewards of autonomy in their work, if only on a modest scale, is equally important. Staff deserve to be challenged and trained to use independent judgment and to share a sense of responsibility and ownership of the program. Good work experiences may form the basis for future career choices and do influence the delivery of service to the community. The true goals of college librarianship are not being met if current employees or students are attracted to librarianship as a future career because they perceive the work to be safe from the turmoil of society, routine, and non-demanding. If these beliefs are reinforced by the libraries they experience as students and workers, librarianship will suffer. Intellectually demanding, stimulating, and energetic library directors, library faculty, and staff give true benefit to the library and the profession. Their actions can make librarianship attractive to the best and the brightest undergraduates. The task may begin with a redesign of the jobs held by student library employees to strengthen their content to include responsibilities commensurate with their talents. Mentoring these student employees and working with the college career center and library schools to generate interest in, and publicize the rewards of, librarianship can promote the recruitment of excellent candidates.

CONTRIBUTIONS OF STAFF

Good library staffs bring libraries to life. Poorly trained and ineffectively motivated staff can severely damage a library's program. An exemplary human resources management program develops and accommodates excellent library employees and provides them with unbiased position classification, adequate compensation and benefits, recognition of merit, and a system that encourages job mobility and advancement.

Traditionally, human resources management has been the province of the library director, who was the only one responsible for establishing the library's personnel plan and setting major policies and procedures. It was anticipated that employees would passively accept assignments, working conditions, and benefits. The emergence of a highly educated work force and new theories about management have led to increased participation and cooperation in generating individual and group goals and policies for institutions.

In general, those called librarians are responsible for planning and developing new programs, and for assigning the execution and maintenance of ongoing programs to others. Librarians and other professionals are expected to apply theory and leadership to the solutions of problems. Support staff are responsible for applying learned procedures to the solution of repetitive problems and for participating in the design of solutions for problems that emerge. A job classification system should provide guidelines to help clarify roles and distinguish between library tasks. Yet, blurring between professional and support tasks seems inevitable. In some libraries, for instance, distinctions between professionals and support staff are effaced when experienced employees who lack formal credentials head a periodicals, acquisitions, or circulation department. The traditional department that has five faculty members with Ph.D.s and one secretary who is a high school graduate can be much clearer about the distinct roles assigned to faculty and support staff than can a library, particularly a library with a well-educated support staff. Another factor that makes library staffing more complex is that much of the clerical work in libraries requires special knowledge and is often more difficult and demanding than what is assigned to support staff in other parts of the college community. The presence of large numbers of student employees who may work as little as five hours a week and yet will be called upon to speak for the library in some encounters with the library's public adds a third dimension of staffing challenge.

Staffing patterns in the library are poorly understood by the rest of the campus. Users are unlikely to differentiate clerical from professional staff, bringing equal expectations to the person at the desk. Administrators are unlikely to distinguish between the demands made by library work on library assistants and the demands made on support staff in other parts of the campus.

Insufficient clerical assistance accounts for a substantial portion of the lack of distinction between professional and support staff, and makes more understandable the campus confusion about the role of librarians. The ratio of clerical to librarian positions in academic libraries has hovered around two to one, despite strong recommendations from professional organizations that more clerical employees are needed, and that the ratio be closer to three to one. John Minter Associates, using National Center for Educational Statistics data, reports that the median number of librarians and other professionals employed in a sample of college and university libraries in 1992 was twelve, comprising 27.59 percent of total staff. In 1985, a typical college had ten librarians on the staff and fourteen support staff, a substantial increase over 1970-71, when the comparable figures were 6.9 professionals and 9.4 support staff.[3] On the average, colleges also hire thirty thousand hours of student help—the equivalent of sixteen full-time employees—during a year. When student and clerical positions are combined, the total number of support staff employees reaches thirty, and produces a ratio of support staff to librarians that is considerably closer to the ideal. Since student employees are rarely trained to perform the full range of tasks done by other staff, this manipulation of the ratio is not completely satisfactory. However, it is a salutary reminder that student employees deserve to be counted and need to be well utilized if the cost of hiring them is to be justified.

Ratios of professional to other library employees only reveal part of the staff story. The other important component is the amount spent for salaries, wages, and benefits, in comparison with materials and other expenditures of the library. Recent formulas suggest that the ratio to describe the relationship between these categories should approximate 60:30:10.[4] Current practice is somewhat different. A recent study of quality liberal arts college libraries revealed that the average salary costs have claimed about 44 percent of the library budget, with materials at 38 percent and other operating expenses at 17.5 percent.[5] Raising the personnel budget of a library at the expense of materials is and will remain difficult. Despite the fact that professional staff cost ratios are substantially lower for the library than they are for the remainder of the institution, it is nonetheless uncomfortable for college administrators to witness growth in the library personnel budget when they consider acquiring materials, not staff, as the library's real objective. That ever-present tension mandates that library directors frame staff choices in terms that are understandable to administrators and cause them to link library programs with both staff and material costs rather than merely to categorize budgets into staff, materials, and other expenditures.

Building on the talents of individual staff members is a practical necessity for college libraries with small staffs where all the required tasks can only be accomplished by assigning them to staff members who can best perform them, whatever their job description. Small staffs permit a large degree of autonomy, variety, innovation, and flexibility to be applied to the construction of most jobs. Combining attention to individual strengths, with adherence to the principles of job design, performance evaluation, participatory management, and staff development, gives a library the best opportunity to develop a quality work environment. The "compleat" librarian, a relatively new concept, is expected to accept responsibilities in both public and technical services, to have a broader background, and be willing to participate holistically in the entire library, rather than only in some of its parts. Similarly, libraries that develop mechanisms for staff in several departments to work together to accomplish certain tasks also utilize the "compleat" staff member model.

Contrary to notions of colleges as ivory towers, ivy-covered retreats from an uncivilized world, today's campuses are fiercely competitive. Arguments are waged about virtually every aspect of academic life, and academics are good debaters. Skilled librarians learn how to mount strong cases, develop consensus, build coalitions, and mobilize support on campus. Translating a larger vision into a plan of action for a new program, preparing the documentation, devising a tentative budget, and presenting it convincingly in a proper forum is one of the most challenging and rewarding tasks of a college librarian. One task that offers a myriad of opportunity is hiring new staff. The opportunity for supporting change is present as a slate of candidates presents different talents. If ensuring the viability of the library in the future is a concern, each new hire offers the opportunity to seek out risk takers and other individuals with different types of competencies, including interpersonal and training skills. Affirmative action can also guide the successful recruitment of new employees in college libraries. It is not unusual for advertisements to contain phrases such as "the college is an equal opportunity employer and welcomes applications from minorities and women." Librarians should welcome strategies that encourage entry to the profession of all qualified applicants, regardless of racial or cultural background, rather than bemoan what they perceive to be rigid quotas or mandatory search procedures. The current composition of most library staffs in no way reflects the composition of the college community, much less the composition of the society at large.[6]

CONDITIONS OF EMPLOYMENT

Librarians and other staff seek to work in an atmosphere that makes them feel they are significant and valuable members of the college's educational establishment. Personnel practices of the library can help to reinforce or negate an employee's sense of worth. Clear, careful articulation of the library's personnel policies and practices suggests professional treatment. A library's policies are further legitimated if they represent the collective efforts of the professional staff who have struggled with the nuances and problems of creating fairness and equity. Codification, in the form of a published document laying out policies governing librarians' conditions of employment, provides further evidence of the importance attributed to library positions. If a campus personnel department agrees to allow a variation of its standard practice to accommodate the needs of the library, the unique agreement needs to be documented in memos to the file.

Policies that require definition are conditions for appointment, promotion, nonrenewal, and change of position. Institutions that offer librarians tenure as a faculty member generally adopt evaluation criteria similar to those used to assess teaching faculty and establish a program of peer review, although there may be variations in the criteria and the review process that address particular responsibilities of librarians. In institutions where faculty status is not granted, librarians need to develop and delineate in writing performance evaluation policies, and include a statement regarding peer review. Grievance procedures, if they exist, are spelled out and academic freedom rights explained. Policies regarding access to leave, travel funds, and continuing education are included, as are statements regarding correlative expectations that librarians will engage in further training and participate in the scholarly and professional life of their field. The college personnel office is expected to provide written descriptions of benefit programs—retirement annuities, insurance, hospitalization, sick leave. If library support staff differ in status and benefits from clerical staff in other parts of the college, they should receive a similar document.

Salary is the major source of income for most librarians. Therefore, an individual college library's ability to compete for high-quality staff is influenced greatly by its salary schedule, its package of fringe benefits, and how it compares in other aspects with similar institutions. Library directors, working with personnel managers, bear responsibility for developing a systematic approach to salary administration and for establishing broad classes of positions reciprocally related to a salary schedule that undergoes continual review. The minimum objective of such an approach should be to offer librarians and other staff salaries competitive with similar libraries in the region, annual increases at least equal on a percentage basis with other campus salaries, and merit increases based on a continuing evaluation of each individual's work. In the absence of firm information about the remuneration of local faculty, some data can be gathered using the annual salary survey conducted by AAUP and reported in *Academe* and the *Chronicle of Higher Education*.[7]

Library salary information is available from any number of sources. The American Library Association's Office for Research and Office for Library Personnel Resources publishes one such survey, ARL another.[8] Some state library associations offer salary guidelines and the *Library Journal* lists starting salaries each year. Library directors at comparable institutions are generally willing to share basic information about salary ranges and classification systems.

Compensation includes more than salaries. Fringe benefits can represent as much 30 percent of a salary package. Library staff generally receive many of the same benefits as other members of the college community. Due to a recent change in federal law, institutions of higher education are now compelled, if they wish to offer a benefit, to make the same benefits available to similar categories of employees. As a result, in the private college sector that offers their employees tuition exchange programs or tuition benefits for offspring, the programs are now more accessible to all college employees, although different periods of service and waiting periods can be required to establish eligibility for different categories of employee groups. Similarly, colleges must offer equitable pension plans to all personnel.[9]

Library staffs are not typically highly paid. Salary considerations did not govern the choice most librarians made to join the profession. They chose the work for its importance, its inherent interest, or for a variety of other reasons, and accepted the trade-offs implicit in making their decision. However, passivity in the face of declining individual purchasing power when salaries do not even keep pace with inflation is inappropriate behavior. Library directors and librarians should inform themselves about the dimensions of faculty and staff compensation on their own campuses as well as nationally in order to mobilize the best possible case for the adequate remuneration of all staff.

Information about salary practices in allied fields and remedial compensation strategies can provide library directors with ammunition to assist them in arguing for improved levels of support for library staff. Comparable worth, or pay equity, the concept that salaries of men and women in fields that are comparable should be roughly equivalent, has been helpful in raising salaries for librarians and library staff at some institutions.[10] Professional literature suggests that libraries devote up to 10 percent of their total personnel budgets on staff development.[11] However, a recent survey revealed that for most college libraries the allocation remains at less than 1 percent. The absence of expenditure does not always indicate that activities supporting staff training and enhancement are totally ignored. Supervision and mentoring are aspects of staff development. So, too, are access to sabbaticals and paid or even unpaid leaves for educational, professional, or scholarly purposes.

Librarians working in small colleges suffer from a kind of intellectual and professional isolation, caused perhaps by the college's geographic location or alternately by the pressure of daily work; either may act as a deterrent to staff interaction with librarians at other institutions. Directors and staff alike require opportunities to alleviate this dissociation. Encouraging participation in association work is one method; supporting research and advanced study is another approach; helping staff develop workshops is yet another tactic. Finally, establishing a procedure to ensure that staff will regularly read and discuss professional material guarantees that they will remain current with improvements and events in the field.

ETHICAL RELATIONS OF LIBRARIANS

Professions, as distinct from occupations or trades, are characterized by formal training in a field whose core is a cognitive body of knowledge, the development of skills relating to this knowledge, and an institutional framework controlling the application of those skills. A code of ethics that defines the relationship between the individual or group and the society, and to each other, is an integral part of a profession's social ethos. Two important American Library Association documents form the ethical base from which all librarians operate: the *Code of Ethics* and the *Library Bill of Rights*. The first focuses on the responsibilities of librarians to each other and to the agencies in which they are employed.[12] The other stresses the rights of library users to receive information from all points of view and the obligation of librarians to supply it.[13]

Librarians have a responsibility to be honest stewards of the resources entrusted to their care, to be fair in their dealings with all individuals, employees, coworkers, and library users, to speak out in support of the rights of individuals to access to information, and to insure the confidentiality of library circulation records. Most college librarians will not have to contend, as did Columbia University and many others, with requests from the FBI to search circulation records to determine whether any alleged spies have checked out materials. On the other hand, college libraries are regularly asked by faculty and students to reveal who has borrowed a particular book. While less common, it is not unusual for faculty to request circulation librarians to allow them to see the borrowing records of a particular student in order to help identify plagiarized materials. A decision about whether to purchase a controversial item should be based on merit and need, not pressure from a campus faction. Attempts to censor college library materials must be met with resistance, and principles of academic freedom vigorously defended. Librarians participating in discussions of social issues have a duty to distinguish between their social responsibilities as citizens and their social responsibilities as librarians.

Care must be taken not to permit an "ends justifies the means" attitude to prevail when setting policies and determining goals. The need to retrench, for instance, requires honest and realistic appraisal of priorities. Collection development decisions should be based on objective criteria, not coercion by aggressive faculty. Attaching undue importance to numbers of library holdings leads to dubious methods of counting, to abandonment of book selection principles, or to inadequate weeding. Overinfatuation with library statistics of all kinds brings with it the danger of emphasizing quantity rather than quality of performance.

Ethical conduct in personnel matters requires librarians to judge employees fairly and not let professional rivalries or personal bias intrude on decisions. Librarians must not permit the needs of the library to impede an employee's progress. Promotions should be granted even when this may mean a temporary loss of sufficient personnel for a particular department. Similarly, requests for professional references should be met honestly and be reliable, objective, and free from bias. With the opening of personnel files, letters of reference have grown more generous and, thus, less reliable. It is tempting to wax eloquent about the few good virtues of an inadequate staff member whose presence on the staff is a constant irritant. Needless to say, such a response is unethical.

Librarians, too, have responsibilities to the library and the institution. Except when circumstances are intolerable, librarians have an obligation to remain in a position long enough to have achieved definite results before considering a move. Training on any job is expensive, and benefits to the employer do not begin to accrue for some time after a new employee has joined the staff. While the time period may vary with the position and the institution, two years is considered a minimum. Common courtesy calls for librarians actively considering another position to discuss their plans with the director. When a true decision to leave has been made, librarians owe their directors at least two or three months before departure, and if possible, should arrange to have their leave-taking coincide with the end of the semester.

Just as college librarians accept the responsibility to behave in an ethical manner toward their community, the community has the same obligation to behave ethically toward its librarians. Library directors must often protect staff from attacks, particularly by faculty requesting special privileges. Defending the rights of the library and its employees in these situations can be difficult and unpleasant, and may require appeal to the highest authorities in the college. Library employees have a right to expect this level of loyalty and support from their directors.

SUMMARY

College library directors and library staffs have broad latitude to impose their visions and value systems on the institutions they lead and serve, and thereby to shape them into environments that foster and stimulate good teaching and learning. Sharing their vision with members of the user community helps gain acceptance for the library's program. Library directors have a special obligation to support field-wide library values and norms of behavior.

Without competent staff, a good library collection languishes and the college loses the benefit of its investment. The goal of human resources management, the term currently used to describe personnel work, is to make certain that all employees are treated fairly and that they remain motivated to perform good work. Libraries are among the civilizing institutions in our society and their treatment of employees should reflect that orientation.

NOTES

1. Joanne Euster, *The Academic Library Director: Management Activities and Effectiveness* (New York: Greenwood Press, 1987), passim.

2. Cliff Glaviano and R. Errol Lam, "Academic Librarians and Affirmative Action: Approaching Cultural Diversity in the 1990's," *College and Research Libraries* 51(November 1990): 512-13; Rick B. Forsman, "Incorporating Organizational Values into the Strategic Planning Process," *Journal of Academic Librarianship* 16 (July 1990): 151.

3. John Minter, *Statistical Norms for College and University Libraries* (Boulder, Colo.: John Minter Assoc., 1994); Association of College and Research Libraries, *Library Statistics of Colleges and Universities, 1985: National Summaries, State Summaries, Institutional Tables* (Chicago: ACRL, 1987). Data on three thousand academic libraries from 1985 Higher Education General Information Survey (HEGIS) study of National Center for Educational Statistics (NCES). Note: federal survey by NCES is now called IPEDS after new title Integrated Postsecondary Education Data System)

4. Patricia Senn Breivik and E. Gordon Gee, *Information Literacy: Revolution in the Library* (New York: American Council on Education and Macmillan, 1989), 112.

5. Richard Hume Werking, "Collection Growth and Expenditures in Academic Libraries: A Preliminary Inquiry," *College and Research Libraries* 52 (January 1991): 8.

6. Office for Library Personnel Resources, American Library Association,

Academic and Public Librarians Data by Race, Ethnicity, and Sex, 1986. (Chicago: American Library Association, 1986). Also summarized in *Library Personnel News* 5 (January/February 1991): 5.

7. "Annual Report on the Economic Status of the Profession, 1990-91," *Academe* 7 (March/April, 1990): 9-90 and *Chronicle of Higher Education* 38 (April 1990) 1+.

8. Mary Jo Lynch, Margaret Myers and Jeniece Guy, *ALA Survey of Librarian Salaries, 1990* (Chicago: American Library Association, 1990).

9. Teachers Insurance and Annuity Association-College Retirement Equities Fund (TIAA-CREF), *Getting Your Plan in Shape* (New York: TIAA-CREF, 1988); TIAA-CREF, *Keeping Your Plan in Shape* (New York: TIAA-CREF, 1991); *Benefits Plan Counselor*, 1980-to present, a newsletter published by TIAA-CREF.

10. Carolyn Kenady, *Pay Equity: An Action Manual for Library Workers* (Chicago: American Library Association, 1989); *Pay Equity Issues and Strategies, vol.9, Topics in Personnel* (Chicago: Office for Library Personnel Resources, American Library Association, 1986).

11. Charles Martell and Richard Dougherty as quoted in Jana Varlejs, "Cost Models for Staff Development in Academic Libraries," *Journal of Academic Librarianship* 12 (January 1987): 360.

12. Lee W. Finks, "Librarianship Needs a New Code of Ethics," *American Libraries* 22 (January 1991): 86.

13. American Library Association, *Intellectual Freedom Manual*, 3d. ed. (Chicago: American Library Association, 1989): 14.

Chapter 9

PLANNING ISSUES

Fiscal stewardship, facilities management, and program evaluation are elements of planning germane to the tasks of each member of the library staff. Each area offers scope for specialization in librarianship; each area also tends to be glossed over as not relevant to the tasks of a line librarian. This is not true. Each individual employed in the library should have some understanding of the fiscal, functional, and service components of the library. Some employees may need to comprehend significant work in one or more of these areas if they are to develop measures of effectiveness or ensure efficiency as part of a job or committee assignment.

BUDGETS

Academic deans provide leadership about budget priorities; treasurers document the college's financial state. Although financial officers must oversee and ensure the fiscal integrity of an institution, their duties do not generally include judging the merit of a particular budget request, or granting it final approval. This responsibility belongs to the chief academic officer although in many colleges, a select group of faculty review budgets in terms of their relationship to campus priorities. Using information about previous and current income and expenditure, these actors set future budgets.

Relationships with both faculty and administrators who work on the budget are important to the library. Winning a sound financial bases for the library requires the successful performance of two important tasks. The first is to establish rational and mutually satisfying relationships and procedures to accommodate campus officers who handle the library's financial affairs. The second is to develop cost-effective, convincing, and defensible budgets. The budget goal is to relate the financial needs of the library to the library's goals and objectives in a clear and convincing fashion. At any given time, budget events may overlap. Annual budgets are developed one full year in advance of implementation, during a period when money is being spent from a budget that was approved the previous year. Throughout the course of a year, librarians may be required to create, in addition to an annual budget, project budgets for capital expenditures and grant applications or retrenchment budgets relating to a variety of scenarios. One potentially salutary by-product of the recent decline in funding is that libraries, along with other parts of the academic community, have begun to pay stricter attention to issues of financial planning, cost-benefit studies, alternative budget models, and the dynamics of budget presentation. As a budget center serving the entire campus, the library makes its choices about what to recommend for funding with attention to equity across departments as well as concern for costs. Choices become more visible when they are linked to reduced allocations, and the politics of seeking support can intensify.

SOURCES OF INCOME

Three main sources fund the library. The principal source is an appropriation from the current operating budget of the college. The other two sources are grants and gifts. Adequate allocations for colleges depend most heavily first on the general availability of funds. Presidents and budget committees have only a small amount of discretionary money to allocate each year. If the college is fortunate enough to have a sizable endowment, it will be able to support some of its operating budget with income from endowment investments; if not, tuition and fees will be the primary source of revenue for the college, and all expenses will have to be met from this source, perhaps supplemented by grants and gifts to the college.

Most privately controlled colleges have endowment funds specifically designed for the library. In older, well-established institutions, these funds may be substantial, but many colleges receive only a small income from any alternate income sources.[1] The larger and less restrictive the endowment, the more useful it is to the library. Development offices generally work closely with the library director to attract endowment gifts and to help establish guidelines for their use. Most college libraries set a minimum size of five thousand dollars for a named endowment, but the amount varies with the general fortunes of the library. Planning and implementing a program of sustained giving through the creation of endowments is an important component of the library's financial plan.[2] Seeking alternative funding sources is a recent development for many directors. Libraries pursuing outside funding sources will need to be clear about needs, committed to sustaining a development program, farsighted in the design of fund-raising strategies, and willing to compile objective measures of success.[3]

Grants from foundations are another potential source of nonappropriated income. Both local and national foundations are often willing to fund library building programs, library automation efforts, or the establishment of collections to support one or more newer areas of the curriculum. A local foundation that agrees to finance a new professor and program in Near Eastern studies may also be willing to consider granting the library seed money to build the collection in that area. The articulate, visible library director can convince development officers that library materials are needed to support any new program, so that as grants are being developed, a sum is included for their purchase. Librarians are expected to gather information documenting need that development officers can use to shape a proposal and to give informed briefings to foundation officials who make campus visits. Foundation giving is an important source of support, particularly for private colleges. Alert directors maintain an interest in foundations that regularly grant funds to college libraries. The activities of major foundations who support libraries can be located in the *Bowker Annual*, annual reports of foundations, and the *Foundation Directory*.

Various state and federal agencies also fund library-related programs. The purposes of grants administered by these agencies is generally tied to national and state educational goals, and can range from increasing retention rates of minority students to wiring the campus for newer technologies. Governmental agencies establish sets of procedures to follow when making application for grants. Often complicated, they almost always entail a substantial amount of paperwork. Before embarking on the application process, it is well to ensure that the central program being promoted in the grants is one that supports the mission of the library, and that there is a fit between the college's agenda and the guidelines of the funding body. Preliminary conversations with the staff of the grant agency prior to application can help to avoid needless effort. Small grant applications, ones that require little preparation and make limited demands on staff time, are not a problem. Grants entailing major investments of time and effort to prepare, and mandating excessive commitments for implementation are only sought when their goals fit well with those of the library. All libraries desire the support that comes from external funding agencies, but care should be taken to avoid any unanticipated and deleterious side effects.[4] Gifts to the library can be viewed in the same manner. Collection development policies usually call out the rights of the accepting library to use or discard the gift books as needed, but the larger issues of solicitation of material gifts do call for some analysis of the process of potential donor identification and solicitation in cost-benefit terms. Random acceptance of collections is foolish, given the costs of collection maintenance, but practicing acts of kindness to those cleaning out personal libraries may enrich a future book sale and garner support for the college library's collection development program.

BUDGET AND EDUCATION AND GENERAL EXPENDITURES

Standards for College Libraries recommends that a minimum of 6 percent of the educational and general expenditures (E&G) portion of the college budget be allocated to libraries. In the most selective colleges, the figure often exceeds—sometimes by several percentage points—the recommended minimum. In 1994, the median education and general expenditures for libraries was 5 percent in publicly supported bachelor-1-degree-granting institutions of higher education, 3 percent in bachelor-2 types, and 3 percent in private bachelor-degree-granting 1 and 2 institutions. The majority of all institutions have not achieved a 5 percent level of education and general expenditures for their libraries. The 95th percentile for public bachelor-degree-granting institutions is 6 percent and 4 percent for private-level 1; private-level 2 is 4 percent.[5] In the 1993-94 budget year, $173 billion were expended on higher education.[6] These dollar figures, while impressive in the aggregate, offer little solace to library directors faced with the difficult task of increasing the library's share of the education budget by even as little as one-tenth of a percent. Proportions allocated to various college library services do not change easily. Indeed, over time, the library may have seen its share diminish in the face of more pressing campus needs, such as the development of a technological infrastructure or the strengthening of the admissions or development offices. Given the campus competition for available funds, library budget documents represent the most important short-term planning statement of the library. In most cases, they are also viewed as opportunities for political persuasion.

The budget is an estimate of amounts of money the library will require during the coming year or biennium in order to carry out its program. A difficult exercise at best, if the budget must be drawn up several years in advance of disbursement, as some state colleges require, the task of estimating financial need for specific programs is even more arduous. The director will have to remind college financial officers and others that the budget is an *estimate* of what will be required to purchase books, equipment, and staff, and that changes within categories between the time of the budget's creation and its execution may be necessary. No two college library directors will prepare the same budget. Variations result from differing college missions, the history of the library, college practices with respect to charge-backs for physical plant and other services, and the budget development guidelines of the college.

BASICS IN BUDGET MAKING

Library directors have primary responsibility for preparing the library budget. Prior to its submission, they will have consulted with library staff, especially department heads, and held discussions with the library committee and the dean. Librarians are fortunate when they work in an institution where the cycle of budget request, budget approval, and budget implementation permits them sufficient lead time to recruit new staff or design appropriate procedures after the request for new funds has been granted.

Previous years' budgets and expenditure statements form part of the database necessary to compile a new budget. Typically, forms distributed by colleges for budgets are arranged by line item, with such categories as personnel, fringe benefits, supplies, equipment, and materials called out in a predictable order and identified by codes unique to the college library and accompanied by a blank to fill in the requested information. Once the nonnegotiable items are identified, then attention is turned to identifying budget categories where changes are desirable or at least negotiable. Even apparently fixed-cost items may have some variability, and these should be considered, as well. For example, the number of hours the library is open is subject to increase or decrease. Imposing a change in either direction will require more or fewer dollars to pay staff for service.

The assumption underlying all budget discussions is that the library serves a public good, and is, in effect, the best and most cost-effective agency to provide information options for the entire community. Ann

Prentice suggests that the social contract that affirms these assumptions may not be as firmly or securely established on college campuses as librarians believe it to be. Reasserting its centrality may become increasingly important in the future as more alternate, often private, information agencies develop.[7]

New programs are expected to be fully described and costed out, and possible savings from other parts of the budget allocated to them. This approach represents a modified version of program budgeting. The library's standard programs are those of acquiring materials, organizing them for use, and disseminating and interpreting them through activities of circulation, administration, reference and bibliographic instruction. Linking these functional areas of the library to the changing goals of the college is equally important to budget preparation, even if the documentation is abbreviated. New curricular thrusts of the college, for instance, will find echoes in the library's budget. The final set of commonly agreed-on priorities, usually a mix of ongoing and new programs, becomes the budget.

The requirements for budget presentation will differ from campus to campus. A fortunate director is given the opportunity to present the budget in person to a review group. In colleges where faculty participate in budget determination, they will form part of the team to be educated and convinced. The director's goal for the budget presentation is to demonstrate how essential the library is to the academic program. A clear, well-documented description, with time allowed for a question and discussion period furthers the effort. All too often, the budget goes directly to the dean, and the decision is unilateral, or solely an administrative one. While the text of the final budget document may include comparative data about relative support given to libraries of similar institutions, the soundest approach to justifying the budget estimates is careful description and analysis of the library's own activities and needs. Whether the presentation is made to a committee or a single administrator, the need for copious attention to detail and justification remains essential.

The same principles of budgeting apply whether the document in preparation is a routine annual budget or a capital one designed to support a major effort—an integrated library system or a remodeling project, for instance. The request document must be linked to the goals of the college, should outline the program elements, estimate their respective costs, offer a timetable for implementation, and describe the impact that positive or negative decision will have.

The principal parts of the library budget are salaries, materials, and other operating expenses. While recommendations vary about the proper percentages to allot to each of these categories, a 60-30-10 breakdown—60 percent staff, 30 percent materials, and 10 percent other—has frequently been suggested. The proportions deviate from institution to institution, based, in part, on current financial exigencies, past history, and book endowment funds. In general libraries, even when full automated, are labor-intensive operations, and so staffing is a large component for most academic libraries. The trend appears to be irreversible and may be responsible for the heightened importance accorded to funding access to materials and for articulating that need in budget allocations that make it possible to deliver documents to patrons in a timely fashion.

Within the materials budget, further decisions about allocation ratios—between, for instance, monographs and periodicals—are necessary. While some libraries spend two-thirds or more of their budgets on serials, the median during the past ten years has fluctuated between 45 percent and 57 percent.[8] A college that does not use formula budgeting for the materials budget may find it fruitful to develop alternate ways to describe the relationships between expenditures for staff, materials, and operating expenses. One approach is to cluster costs into categories of use by program.

The ultimate financial responsibility of the library director and other members of the library faculty and staff can be described as a stewardship. Each employee has some responsibility to use the college's current resources in a manner that protects its investment in the future.

TECHNOLOGY PLANNING

Librarians active in the field in the late 1960s remember the tasks associated with the introduction of OCLC in their library as the first large-scale technological effort in their careers. Some systems librarians from that period also participated in the development of the first online public access catalogs, while pioneering librarians in the 1970s experienced the challenge of selecting and installing first- and second-generation commercially developed OPAC software. Still earlier, library technology planning included the work done to develop large-scale microform sets, cooperative microfilming projects, and the testing of microform at equipment and other reprographic equipment. For any new technology there are early, middle, and late adoption cycles as institutions and individuals position themselves at the forefront, middle, or end of the technology innovation line. Decisions to introduce technology are made on the basis of the usefulness of the technology to certain tasks and the importance of the tasks to the operation. Questions and answers about cost, reliability, critical mass, and ease of use all influence the cycle of adoption on a given campus.

Technology-planning efforts need to provide for periods of brainstorming, preliminary goal development, allocation of learning tasks, learning time, refinement of goals, education of others, budget development, seeking of funding, purchasing, installation, publicity, and education of users.

Teamwork and its corollary, coordination are assumed in college library technology efforts. It is rare for one librarian to have all the talents called for in a full implementation effort or to be performing the work in isolation. New work styles may have to be learned and performance evaluation may now be based on team efforts. In some cases, the details of the project demand the extra attention; in others, the installation is relatively straightforward, but the funding issues are demanding, and in still others, it is the politics of the project that call for extra care. Modifications to the traditional budget arrangements occur as librarians seek ways to increase the amount of budget dollars allocated to electronic access options to alleviate some of the financial pressures of inflation and declining bases of local support for traditional library services.

Short of an endowment for innovation, they must find ways to reallocate current dollars. To do so successfully, they must educate campus leaders, faculty, and students to understand that the relationships between electronic databases, expanding the regular collection, and providing services (including reference, collection management and circulation) are dynamic, not static. Priorities need to be selected and honored that best meet the needs of the college community in the future.

Asking users to identify their needs and preferences can assist in the transition period from exclusively print collections to hybrid collections. In many cases, users desire electronic databases and auxiliary services such as the ability to download or print out articles for a modest fee. However, some disciplines rely more heavily on the monograph as the medium of communication and find electronic databases a secondary source of scholarship. One service that the library must provide is to speak from experience about the multiple paths users have when searching for knowledge and design systems that honor diversified approaches to information seeking. In this way, the library can maintain its reputation for providing quality service while exerting leadership in the design and delivery of new campus information service options.

THE LIBRARY BUILDING AND EQUIPMENT

Constructing a new academic library building, or renovating or adding to an old one, is a very expensive undertaking. It is therefore essential that the process of planning and equipping the library be done efficiently and economically. Although a variety of reasons may account for why a college community finds an existing library building less functional—changing patterns of use, for instance, or new building standards—but the most urgent cause is generally inadequate size, with growth in the collections as the key pressure point. Diminished capacity to house new acquisitions is never a sudden event, but is the result of incremental growth tightening. The time to begin thinking about the problem and developing documentation demonstrating the projected inadequacy of the current building is several years before the need is urgent. Many librarians report that decisions to act are not made until several years after space problems are acute.

Librarians who find their present buildings unsatisfactory and have garnered campus support for some form of action have four courses of action open to them. First, they can renovate the existing structure; second, they can build an addition and remodel; third, they can occupy and convert to their needs an existing structure originally designed for another purpose; or, finally, they can erect a totally new building. While librarians may be convinced that their problems will best be solved by a new structure, because of the high costs of a new building, or perhaps because older members of the faculty and alumni are very attached to the existing library, or because of other campus financial exigencies, the question of whether it is feasible to renovate or enlarge an existing building is often raised. Each institution must arrive at its own solution. At this point, the library staff's obligation is to insure that the decision is based on adequate consideration of all the factors involved. The best approach to providing sufficient information on which to make a judgment is to undertake a needs assessment. A needs assessment has two elements: what is required and what exists. The comparison between the two should reveal whether a new library is called for or whether one of the other options can be adopted.

NEEDS ASSESSMENT TEAM

The first step in any needs assessment is to organize a needs assessment team. This may be an expanded library committee, or may be what will later become the building committee. The importance of this group is confirmed by appointing to it respected representatives from the college administration, faculty, and student body, a building consultant, if there is one, and, of course, the library director. Appointing members with varied backgrounds, different academic disciplines, and diverse types of expertise enhances its usefulness. As users of the library, faculty, and students are, more often than not, unfamiliar with or indifferent to the details of its technical services operations, they will require careful coaching and orientation about them. Placing a library-minded trustee on the committee can help facilitate communications with the board of trustees about the library's needs and influence their willingness to provide financial support to the project. While the committee should be representative, there is a danger of it growing too large. On the other hand, since those serving on the committee become advocates of the program, limiting numbers also limits vocal support.

It is the job of the needs assessment team to review library goals, evaluate existing conditions, examine alternatives to a new building, determine objectives for the new space, decide its space requirements, and prepare a document for presentation to the administration, trustees, and other community members. The components of a needs assessment statement include collections, in all formats, reader facilities, library staffing, and the capacity of existing building space to accommodate change and projected growth. Much of the work of the needs assessment team must be repeated from a somewhat different perspective by the planning team. This is one compelling reason for the same team to function in both capacities. For instance, the needs assessment group will consider what changes, if any, are projected for academic programs and whether it is anticipated that the size of the population to be served will change. The answers to both of these questions will have some impact on whether additional library space is required. The planning committee will use the information to help write the building program, described below.

The needs assessment documents objectives for the library and user services, and should explain the library and its organization, within the context of the existing structure. It should, therefore, describe the collection and new technology, and consider the scope and nature of the need for flexibility in light of expected changes and how the old building is to be used. For instance, the three following statements might appear:

1. The building must be organized and designed so that it is user-oriented.
2. The library must collect, house and service all materials needed by users.
3. New space must accommodate technology.

Specific objectives regarding collection growth, services, and reader accommodations will be developed for the building program. A number of factors determine the answer about whether to remodel, renovate, or build anew. Among them are obsolescence, inefficiency, disruption of service, and other uses for the present building.

PLANNING THE NEW LIBRARY BUILDING

If the decision is "go" on a new library building, the first steps are to organize a planning committee, select an architect, and reach a collective judgment on the important administrative and educational questions that have to be settled before a formal program can be written or a suitable site chosen.

It cannot be stressed too strongly that the library director should take the lead in informing the planning committee of new developments in library building and equipment. Nor can it be stressed strongly enough that this requires careful preparation before any meeting is held. Directors without experience sometimes tend to minimize the amount of effort required to build a new building or to participate in a major renovation.

THE BUILDING CONSULTANT

Most college library directors who undertake to build a new library consider hiring a building consultant mandatory for a variety of reasons. They may need outside support to stand up to influential professors or administrators, and sometimes even architects. They also may require expert advice on new developments, say, in technology. Consultants, by virtue of their experience, can save library staff time, help avoid problems, and protect staff morale. In short, the tyranny of expertise can work to a library's favor. Hiring an outside consultant often has the effect of securing a library advocate, a known authority, who commands respect and whose word carries credence. Richard Boss contends that any project that will cost over fifty thousand dollars, or that is intended to meet the needs of the library for a period of at least five years, requires a building consultant.[9]

Building consultants are generally hired for one of three purposes. (1) As "critics," only briefly involved with the project and usually at milestones in the process. This might include the needs assessment statement, the building program, the schematic or design drawings, and the specifications. (2) As "full consultants," totally involved from start to finish. This advisor sits on the needs assessment and planning committees, goes on site visits, and writes reports. (3) As "mediators," more involved than the critics, but less so than full consultants. They pay frequent visits as the work progresses, and review and advise at all stages. For some librarians, the Metcalf text as revised by Weber and Leighton becomes the equivalent of a second consultant on site.[10]

THE ARCHITECT AND THE LIBRARIAN

A great deal has been written about the selection of an architect, about the interaction between the architect and the librarian, and about potential problems in the relationship. What seems important to stress is that librarians and architects can, and frequently do, work well together, despite reports to the contrary. When problems emerge, they are often generated by the conflicting goals that each has for a new building. Architects look at completed buildings as products of good design, as aesthetically appealing, attractive combinations of stone and mortar. Librarians, on the other hand, want structures that accommodate patrons comfortably, that allow control over collections, and that address security problems.

Sometimes a college needs preliminary or schematic plans to mount a capital-funds drive before the final arrangements are made for planning and financing a new building. For funding purposes, most architects will develop a schematic plan and elevation, rendering a model with an approximate cost estimate, for a set sum or a percentage of their total architectural services fee if they are chosen later as the architects for the building.

Administrative and Educational Problems

After a building committee has been formed, its first task is to try to arrive at some collective opinion about a number of administrative and educational matters. The kinds of administrative and educational problems the planning committee will be called upon to discuss are suggested by the following questions:

1. How many students are to be accommodated in the new library?
2. What is the best available site for the building?
3. What is the college policy regarding the provision of audio-visual aids and other mechanical teaching devices? That is, will they be handled separately by departments or will there be a centralized audiovisual service for all departments and will it be in the library?
4. Will existing departmental collections be absorbed in the new library building?
5. How will the building accommodate new technology?
6. Will the library share its quarters with other activities?

When the building committee has reached a decision on both the objectives of the proposed new library and the administrative and educational problems involved—and only then—is the librarian ready to write a program that intelligently sets forth the requirements the architect will be asked to resolve. Good libraries are designed from the inside out. Library planning is fundamentally a problem-solving activity, and the written program is an important step in that process. Every library building, regardless of its size and function, is unique and should be approached from that standpoint. The purpose of the program is to crystallize thinking about a particular library building and to set forth priorities for it. There are two principal parts: (1) a brief discussion of each of the general conditions that the library staff expects the architect to be aware of in the structural planning of the building; and, (2) a description of the detailed requirements of the purpose, space, and location of each of the areas in the building. General capacities for books and readers, standards for spatial relationships, flexibility, and the like will be called out and then specifics for each primary area will be detailed. In the end, one has the equivalent of a walk through a new building. A systems approach is needed as relationships and interactions between departments must be carefully delineated. The end result is, hopefully, a building that is adequate for its purpose, cost-effective, and capable of offering the users surprise and delight as a result of good design.

SUMMARY

The common factor in budget development, technology implementation, and facilities review is careful and creative planning. Such planning is grounded in an understanding of campus priorities, attitudes towards innovation, and knowledge of previous planning efforts at the college.

Given the relationship of planning to emerging assessment efforts, it is also likely that increasing numbers of staff will have some planning responsibilities. The larger the program being developed the more likely it is that a campus advisory group will share planning responsibility with the library administration. Good planning represents true stewardship of college resources.

NOTES

1. Mary Jo Lynch, *Alternative Sources of Revenue for Academic Libraries* (Chicago, American Library Association, 1991).

2. Betty J. Turock and Andrea Pedolsky, *Creating a Financial Plan* (New York: Neal Schuman, 1992).

3. Victoria Steele and Stephen D. Elder, *Becoming a Fundraiser* (Chicago: American Library Association, 1992).

4. Alice Gertzog, "Gathering Grants— Financial Boom or Bust?," *The Bottom Line,* Charter Issue (1986): 17-20.

5. John Minter, *Statistical Norms for College and University Libraries* (Boulder, Colo.: John Minter Assoc., 1996) (derived from United States Department of Education 1994 Survey of Academic Libraries, known as HEGIS survey).

6. Chronicle of Higher Education, *Almanac of Higher Education,* Sept. 2, 1996 issue, Money (http//Chronicle/merit.edu/almanac/.links.html).

7. Ann Prentice, *Financial Planning for Libraries* (Metuchen, N.J.: Scarecrow Press, 1983): 3-52.

8. Richard Hume Werking, "Collection Growth and Expenditures in Academic Libraries, A Preliminary Inquiry," *College and Research Libraries* 52 (January 1991): 20.

9. Richard W. Boss, *Information Technologies and Space Planning for Libraries and Information Centers* (Boston: G.K. Hall, 1987), 102.

10. George Snowball, "The Building Program-Generalities," in Lester K. Smith, ed. *Planning Library Buildings: From Decision to Design.* Papers from a Library Administration and Management Association Buildings and Equipment Section Preconference at the 1984 American Library Association

Conference, Dallas, Tx. (Chicago, American Library Association, 1986),71-81 and Keyes D. Metcalf, *Planning Academic and Research Library Buildings* 2nd ed. by Philip D. Leighton and David C. Weber (Chicago: American Library Association, 1986).

Chapter 10

EVALUATION

Library evaluation, difficult at best, is made more so because of the elusiveness of the concept "goodness" when used to describe libraries. Even "adequacy" is hard to pin down. Part of the problem stems from the number of ways in which we use the term "goodness." We speak, for instance, about the capability of a library to collect material that meets an articulated need. Or we describe that library's ability to make the information accessible and available so that it can be used. Two kinds of goodness are contained in the above descriptions. One refers to quality and the other to value. In other words, we may ask, How good is a library? (quality) and/or, What good does a library do? (value).[1] A comprehensive collection on the subject of Alaskan kinship systems would undoubtedly contain information needed by a student writing a term paper on the subject. All things being equal, the system is capable of meeting the student's needs. On the other hand, if the student has trouble reading at the level at which most of the books are written, then the holdings are of no value to him.

Evaluation is necessary to any library. It enables librarians to make appropriate decisions particularly about the allocation of resources, to report accurately and in depth to administrators and funding bodies, to demonstrate responsibility and accountability for activities, to diagnose problems in a particular area, to compare programs and activities with like institutions, and to document efforts for the historic record and for longitudinal analysis. Evaluating the effectiveness of a service simply means assessing how well the service meets the demand or needs of the community to be served. At any given time, some library program and/or service should be undergoing scrutiny. But systematic evaluation should never be taken lightly. It is difficult, time consuming, and fraught with dangers that, unless avoided, may harm a library.

What should be evaluated? Everything is appropriate to evaluation and, further, a method can be found to evaluate anything. However, simply data-snooping without focus or clarity of intent produces muddy results. Before embarking on any evaluation, the following important questions must be confronted: What information is required, by whom, and for what purpose? In this way, the decision can be made to evaluate at the appropriate level and to select the method best suited to securing the wanted information. Most evaluations do not *require* the use of computers; however, the ability of computers to process large amounts of information and generate reports rapidly makes using them attractive when there are large quantities of data to be manipulated.

Libraries seeking to evaluate various parts of their operations and programs would do well to consult F. W. Lancaster's *If You Want to Evaluate Your Library*, and Van House, Ward and McClure's *Measuring Academic Library Performance*.[2] Manuals for evaluating specific activities such as reference service or the collection are included when the evaluative considerations for each are discussed.

TYPES OF EVALUATION

The most useful library evaluation assesses the degree to which a library staff meets the goals and objectives that it has set for the library, based on its understanding of the needs of its parent institution and its users; in other words, how a library has performed within its own staff's expectations and aspirations as measured by pre-chosen performance indicators.

In recent years, evaluation in librarianship has moved toward judging effectiveness in terms of the success of users in securing what they are seeking. Performance evaluations always involve: (1) an indication of what constitutes effectiveness or success for the services, the person or the institution to be evaluated; (2) formulated criteria or objectives; (3) criteria translated into measures; (4) data collected using the measures that have been established; and (5) results compared with the definition of effectiveness.[3] Step 6 is synonymous with step 1 and marks the beginning of a new cycle.

Mary Cronin has suggested applying the following five-step performance measurement process to an academic library program: (1) consider possible kinds of measurement based on available or easily collected data; (2) describe user expectations; (3) establish local standards of service; (4) formulate objectives; and, finally, (5) evaluate, or compare the outcome with established standards and user expectations.[4]

The problem, of course, with undertaking an evaluation of the kind described above is that it requires generous commitments of time and staff. For this reason, and sometimes because of fear of the unknown, librarians often opt for less demanding forms of evaluation.

The most frequent type of assessments undertaken by college librarians are counting and comparing inputs. Inputs are such items as the level of support for the library, the number of questions asked of the reference staff, the number of users, number of materials circulated, size of staff, acquisition rates, hours of service, size of building, and periodical holdings. These inputs can then be compared across institutions, or longitudinally for the same institution. Unfortunately, inputs do not correlate reliably with the effectiveness of a program.[5] Outputs, on the other hand, measure use. They look at such variables as circulation per capita or circulation per volume owned, reference questions per capita, and so on. In other words, they report services delivered and uses made of the library. There are caveats to observe when using output measures:

1. Conditions can be manipulated to improve performance on a measure, but not necessarily result in better service.
2. There are no "good" or "bad" scores except as they compare with institutional or service goals.
3. Output measures reflect user success, not simply library performance.[6]

Unfortunately, even with output measures, we are still likely to base judgments about quality and effectiveness only on quantitative results, some of which are immutable, no matter how diligent our attempts to influence and better them. In the absence of qualitative assessment, there is no information about whether students are using library books as doorstops and little insight into whether a reference question has really been addressed or whether the response reflects a librarian's misperception of what the question might have been.

Evaluations can be internal or external, administered by members of the institution or done by others. Some happen automatically. At budget time, for instance, committees review programs. An allocation, while reflecting many factors, probably indicates, at least to some extent, the satisfaction or attitudes of decision makers about the library. Accrediting associations generally ask individual colleges to prepare a self-study that gives as complete a picture as possible of the institution before an accreditation visit. In this situation, the library is usually a component of the self-study and later is reviewed and inspected by the visiting team.

There are other occasions on which the library engages in self-study. Self-study should always precede or be the firm foundation for planning efforts so that the plan finally adopted is based upon a clear sense of a library's strengths and weaknesses. Self-study is often undertaken as a response to a specific, perceived problem, perhaps a space shortage, high staff turnover, or apparent user dissatisfaction. Evaluation is never simply "self," however. If it is to be of use, there must be input from every affected segment of the campus.

A number of aids are available to libraries wishing to undertake a full or partial self-study. The Association of Research Libraries Office of Management Studies has a useful package for mid-sized academic libraries called *The Planning Process for Small Academic Libraries.*[7] Librarians may also want to consult Herbert Kells' *Self Study Processes.*[8]

In recent years, many colleges and universities have embarked on regularly scheduled, periodic evaluations of their academic departments. Libraries, particularly in institutions where they are not considered departments, are generally and unfortunately excluded from the evaluation schedule. The appraisal of the library by an outside expert independent of any accrediting or professional group is usually associated with a particular project—automating services or constructing a new building—or is the result of unhappiness on the part of the library or the college community. Whatever the motivation for calling in an outside consultant, the appraisal should be viewed as an opportunity rather than a threat, and should use the consultant's presence to generate recommendations and suggestions that will enhance the library's position.

STANDARDS

After decades of struggling to devise standards and measures that could be used to evaluate college libraries, most librarians now acknowledge that absolute criteria, universally applicable, are not only nonexistent, but are probably undesirable. Standards, in fact, are not scientifically arrived at quantities or qualities describing excellence, but rather represent minimal norms, based on the statistical means of large numbers of libraries. How a library compares to those norms depends on tradition, wealth, the student body, library leadership, geography, and all of those contextual and environmental elements we have been stressing throughout this book. Standards, misunderstood, can work to the detriment of a college library. An unenlightened administration, for instance, may find justification to reduce a library's budget because its collection or number of staff members exceeds standards. On the other hand, standards do function to establish a bottom point in a library's offerings to a community—building, staff, materials, or services—beneath which libraries may not fall, lest they be judged inadequate in comparison with other institutions, or—perhaps worse—by an accrediting association. In some cases standards do provide the incentive for libraries to develop and grow.

The Middle States Association, one of the regional secondary and higher education accrediting units, has historically stressed a qualitative approach to standards and bases its evaluation on the articulated mission and goals of the college under accreditation review. The library section of the *Characteristics of Excellence in Higher Education: Standards for Accreditation* has nine paragraphs devoted specifically to the college library. The first two read:

> The services, resources and programs of libraries, broadly defined, are fundamental to the educational mission of an institution and to the teaching and learning process. They support the educational program. They facilitate learning and research activities among students, faculty, and staff.
>
> The scope of library/learning resources, the types of services, and the varieties of print and non-print and electronic media depend on the nature of the institution. They must be in reasonable proportion to the needs to be served, but numbers alone are no assurance of excellence. Of more importance are the quality, accessibility, availability, and delivery of resources on site and elsewhere; their relevance to the institution's current programs; and the degree to which they are actually used. The development of services and collections must relate realistically to the institution's educational mission, goals, curricula, size, complexity, degree level, fiscal support, and its teaching, learning, and research requirements.[9]

A new section encourages institutions to foster optimal use of its learning resources through strategies designed to help students develop information literacy; providing concrete evidence of the increasing importance ascribed to this activity. A revised version of the Association of College and Research Libraries *Standards for College Libraries* was published in the April 1995 issue of *College and Research Libraries News.* ACRL *Standards* treat eight topics: objectives, collections, organization of materials, staff, services, facilities, administration, and budget. For each, a standard is given and commentary appended. The standards about collections, staff, and buildings include formulas and procedures for self-grading, and assume a relationship between inputs and quality.[10]

College administrators and accrediting agencies are wary of approaches that present rigid standards that can be manipulated, considering them simultaneously overly subjective and overly dogmatic. Directors should employ them sparingly and with caution.

Making Comparisons

Performance and output measures stress the importance of a library meeting its own goals. On the other hand, being informed about national, local and regional trends, and what peer institutions are doing provides ammunition for budget presentations, reports, grant proposals, and other uses. Benchmarking, a current management technique designed to stimulate the growth of quality services in any industry, suggests the collection of data from institutions the home institution wishes to emulate in a particular area.

The U.S. Department of Education's Office of Educational Research and Improvement's National Center for Educational Statistics biennially collects data on libraries through its Integrated Postsecondary Education Data System (IPEDS) and organizes the data by level of highest degree awarded. The data for 1992 were published in November 1994.[11]

Many helpful statistical reports are generated using the IPEDS data. The Center for Planning Information at Tufts University and John Minter Associates, Inc. in Boulder, Colorado, both reformat the basic data into peer groupings. The non-ARL doctoral granting institutions, known as ACRL University Libraries, also issue statistical information every other year in non-IPEDS years through ACRL. This compilation is modeled on the annual Association of Research Libraries survey.[12]

The Associated Colleges of the Midwest and the Great Lakes College Consortium produce annual compilations of library data for members of the groups, as do other regional associations in the Pacific Northwest and the South. A mix of public and private institutions are

Local computer-based systems provide libraries with information about collection use which was virtually unattainable manually. Information can be collected and tabulated about language, country of origin, publication date, subject (using classification), format, and type of materials being used in the library. Systems can be programmed to monitor, analyze, and project growth, and to help plan for future collection development. Decisions about preservation, storage, and weeding can then be reached less subjectively or intuitively. Computers also render the kind of evaluation that must be made for cooperative acquisitions and resource sharing relatively easy to accomplish.

Computer-based systems also make possible, for the first time, an accurate, detailed picture of library users and nonusers and of the use made of discrete parts of the collection. The categories of patrons who are borrowing what types of materials is readily accessible through automated management-information systems.

Quantitative studies of library use have identified three patterns that have appeared so frequently that they are now referred to as laws: scattering, decay, and inertia. All are manifestations of the law of diminishing returns, and all are useful concepts in library evaluation.

Scattering refers to the use of periodical materials from title to title across a subject. Some materials are used more heavily than others and it is necessary to understand the variations in use of library materials in order to plan what needs to be available to users. Citation analysis, library usage records, and "best" lists have all been useful in determining scattering. S. C. Bradford counted the number of references to each periodical title carrying material about applied geophysics and the literature of automation. Through this method, he identified and ranked the most productive periodicals. A diminishing number of references was contributed by successively less productive periodicals. This became known as "Bradford's Law of Scattering."[13] *Decay* is most easily understood as lessened use over time. Studies have consistently demonstrated that use declines with age,[14] although demand varies widely by subject. The final pattern has been referred to as *inertia*, and describes the decline in library use due to the relative effort required to utilize it. The greater the distance one is from a library, for instance, the greater the effort required to use it. Considerations of "least effort" account for much of library use and nonuse.

Research in academic libraries has tended to focus on the large academic libraries and to emphasize collection development and technology implementation. Survey research in the college library technology implementation. Survey research in the college library environment is often done by teams of practicing college librarians and doctoral candidates with academic library backgrounds. The field has traditionally relied on testimonies of excellent practices rather than examinations of them in a research framework but this tendency is less obvious each year as the practice of framing and answering evaluation questions develops into assessment research.

SUMMARY

Research into procedures, policies, personnel and other aspects of college library service has produced a variety of methods to evaluate and judge how we are doing ,and whether we are doing what we should be. Jane Robbins and Douglas Zweizig named their manual on library evaluation, *Are We There Yet?*[15] to indicate that evaluation should be a process of checking on a regular basis how much progress a library has made toward a stated goal. The importance of systematic evaluation cannot be underestimated. Nor, however, should instinct and educated guesswork. Experienced librarians develop a sixth sense about their institutions. Eyeballing a shelf of books often produces instantaneous knowledge about the degree to which particular information and a subject literature are being utilized. While intuition is never a substitute for formal evaluation, instinct can act as a warning signal and an indication that the time has arrived to initiate a more rigorous examination.

It may be, as Russell Shank contended, that human nature makes one inquisitive so that counting things and arraying the tally in various displays comes with the genes.[16] But data are not information. They must still be analyzed, interpreted, and put to use.

NOTES

1. R. M. Orr, "Measuring the Goodness of Library Services: A General Framework for Considering Quantitative Measures," *Journal of Documentation* 29 (September, 1973): 315-32; Michael Buckland, *Library Services in Theory and Context* (New York: Pergamon Press, 1983), 194-95.

2. F. W. Lancaster, *If You Want to Evaluate Your Library* (Champaign, Ill.: University of Illinois Press, 1988); Nancy Van House, Beth Ward, and Charles McClure, *Measuring Academic Library Performance* (Chicago: American Library Association, 1990).

3. Van House, Ward and McClure, *Measuring Academic.*

4. Mary J. Cronin, *Performance Measurement for Public Services in Academic and Research Libraries*, Occasional Paper 9 (Washington, D.C.: Office of Management Studies, Association of Research Libraries, February 1985).

5. Cronin, *Performance Measurement*, 7.

6. Van House, Ward and McClure, *Measuring Academic*.

7. Duane Webster, *Library Management Review and Analysis Program: A Handbook for Guiding Change and Improvement in Research Library Management* (Washington, D.C.: Association of Research Libraries, 1973); Grady Morein et al., *Planning Process for Small Academic Libraries: An Assisted Self-Study Manual* (Washington, D.C.: Association of Research Libraries, 1980); Grady Morein et al., "The Academic Library Development Program," *College and Research Libraries* 38 (January 1977): 37-45.

8. Herbert Kells, *Self-Study Processes* (New York: MacMillan, 1988).

9. Middle States Association of Colleges and Schools, Commission on Higher Education, *Characteristics of Excellence in Higher Education: Standards for Accreditation* (Philadelphia: Middle States Association of Colleges and Schools, 1994), 15-16.

10. Association of College and Research Libraries, "Standards for College Libraries, 1995 Edition," *College and Research Libraries News* 56 (April 1995): 245-57.

11. National Center for Education Statistics, *Academic Libraries: 1992* (U.S. Department of Education, Office of Educational Research and Improvement, NCES 95-031, November, 1994).

12. Tufts University, Higher Education Data Sharing Consortium [HEDS], IPEDS [*Integrated Post-Secondary Education Data System*] Academic Libraries 1990, Report 90-13 [Private Institutions] (Medford, Mass.: Tufts University, 1990); *Academic Library Statistical Norms 1994* (Boulder, Colo.: John Minter Associates, 1996); Association of College and Research Libraries, *ACRL University Library Statistics 1994-95* (Chicago: Association of College and Research Libraries, 1996).

13. S. C. Bradford, *Documentation* (London: Crosby, Lockwood, 1948).

14. H. H. Fussler and J. L. Simon, *Patterns in the Use of Books in Large Research Libraries* (Chicago: University of Chicago Press, 1969).

15. Jane Robbins and Douglas Zweizig, *Are We There Yet? Evaluating Library Collections, Reference Services, Programs and Personnel* (Madison: School of Library and Information Studies, University of Wisconsin, 1988).

16. Russell Shank as quoted in *Library Automation as a Source of Management Information*, ed. Wilfred Lancaster (Champaign, Ill.: Graduate School of Library and Information Science, University of Illinois, 1982): 2.

Appendix

Standards for College Libraries, 1995 Edition

Final version approved by the ACRL Board and the ALA Standards Committee, February 1995

These standards are intended to apply to libraries supporting academic programs at the bachelor's and master's degree levels. The 1995 edition retains the quantitative approach of the earlier editions. Smaller institutions or those with a strong media services component may find parts of the Standards for community, junior, and technical college learning resources programs useful. Larger institutions or those seeking a more process-oriented approach to standards may find sections of the Standards for University Libraries helpful. The Standards for College Libraries are based historically on practices found at institutions where libraries are providing effective support for the curriculum and for the scholarly and creative accomplishments of students and faculty (Kaser,1982).

The 1995 edition of the standards has the following sections:

Formula A: Collections
Formula B: Librarians
Formula C: Facilities
Bibliography
Committee Members, 1993-95

DEVELOPMENT AND APPROVAL OF THE STANDARDS

The first edition of the *Standards for College Libraries* was published in 1959. Subsequent editions were published in 1975 and 1986. The standards are the particular responsibility of the College Libraries Section Standards Committee, a standing committee of the Association of College and Research Libraries (ACRL), which is a division of the American Library Association (ALA). The College Libraries Section Standards Committee is charged with the responsibility of ongoing review of the standards, consultation with the profession on their development and evaluation and revision as needed. To that end, the committee conducted a national survey in 1991, and the results were reported in the May 1993 issue of *College and Research Libraries* (Walch, 1993). Hearings were held at the 1992 ACRL conference in Salt Lake City, and at the June 1994 ALA conference in Miami. The final version of the 1995 edition was approved by the College Libraries Section Executive Committee, the ACRL Standards and Accreditation Committee, the ALA Standards Committee and the ACRL Executive Board of Directors at the 1995 Midwinter Meeting.

INTRODUCTION

Academic libraries are operating in the midst of extraordinary change in the scholarly communication system. The cost of the traditional system based on paper publication formats is becoming prohibitive, and electronic forms of communication are emerging rapidly. It is too early to tell how much electronic formats will supplant and how much they will only supplement paper formats. These changes raise many questions which will be answered in time. Time is the key; the evolution of this change cannot be predicted with precision. One speculation that seems possible to members of the1993-95 Standards Committee is that the transition will take about thirty years, and we already have gone through the first ten years of the period. In addition to changes in the scholarly communication system, there are many new trends that will change the way effective academic libraries operate. While a few can be recognized now through revisions to the commentaries for the standards, most are not developed well enough to be incorporated into the standards. It is important to be aware of these trends, and they are identified briefly here. The list is not intended to convey priorities.

- Escalating user expectations regarding information retrieval and document delivery times.
- Increased focus on accountability leading to more emphasis on assessment of student performance and interest in output measures as well as input measures.
- "Virtual ownership" in lieu of local, physical ownership; acquiring materials "just in time" instead of "just in case"; title counts becoming more important than volume counts; rapid document delivery through electronic services; degradation of browsing opportunities.
- Stronger emphasis on services to persons with disabilities.
- Shifting patterns in the use of bibliographic utilities; fracturing of the national bibliographic databases; increased importance of networking and development of ANSI standards for search protocols; development of "national information highway".
- Electronic storage and preservation of materials, e.g., reserve reading lists; digitization replacing microforms.
- Traditional audiovisual resources evolving into multimedia and hypermedia.
- Computer equipment pervading library operations and facilities; greater need for staff training and user education in new technologies.
- Emergence of a paraprofessional group of library employees.
- Increased financial pressures for institutions and their libraries.

STANDARDS AND COMMENTARIES

Each standard is followed by commentary intended to amplify its intent and assist in its implementation.

Standard 1: Mission, Goals and Objectives
1.   The college library shall develop an explicit statement of its mission in accord with the mission of the college.
Commentary. It is accepted that the administration and faculty of every college have responsibility to examine the educational program from time to time in light of the goals and purposes of the institution.

Librarians share this responsibility by seeking ways to provide collections and service which support these goals and purposes. Successful fulfillment of this shared responsibility can best be attained when a clear and explicit statement of library mission and goals is prepared and promulgated so that all members of the college community can understand and evaluate the appropriateness and effectiveness of the library program.

1.1 The development of library mission and goals shall be the responsibility of library personnel in consultation with members of the classroom faculty, administrative officers, and students.

Commentary. In developing these missions and goals the library should seek in a formal or structured way the advice and guidance of its primary users, the classroom faculty and students, and of the college administration, in particular those officers responsible for academic programs and policies.

1.2 The statement of library objectives shall be reviewed periodically and revised as necessary.

Commentary. The articulation of library objectives is an obligation of the librarians, with the assistance of the support staff. In reviewing the objectives of the library, careful attention should be paid to ongoing advances in the theory and practice of librarianship. Similarly, changes occurring within the education program of the parent institution should be reflected in a timely way in the program of the library.

Standard 2: Collections

2. The library's collections shall comprise all types of recorded information, including print material in all formats, audiovisual materials, sound recordings, materials used with computers, graphics, and three-dimensional materials.

Commentary. Recorded knowledge and literary or artistic works appear in a wide range of formats. Books represent extended reports of scholarly investigations, compilations of findings, and summaries prepared for institutional purposes. The journal literature communicates more recent information and is particularly important to the science disciplines. Reports in machine-readable form are an even faster means of scholarly communication. Government documents transmit information generated by or at the behest of official agencies, and newspapers record daily activities throughout the world.

Many kinds of communication take place primarily, or exclusively, through such media as films, slidetapes, sound recordings, and videotapes. Microforms are used to compact many kinds of information for presentation and storage. Recorded information also exists in the forms of manuscripts, archives, databases, and computer software packages. Each medium of communication transmits information in unique ways, and each tends to complement the others.

The inherent unity of recorded information and its importance to all academic departments of an institution require that most, if not all, of this information be selected, organized, and made available for use by the library of that institution. In this way the institution's information resources can best be made known and balanced for the benefit of all users.

2.1 The library shall provide as promptly as possible a high percentage of materials needed by its users.

Commentary. The proper development of a collection includes concern for quality as well as quantity. A collection may be said to have quality for its purposes only to the degree that it possesses a portion of the bibliography of each discipline taught, appropriate in quantity both to the level at which each is taught and to the number of students and faculty members who use it. While it is possible to have quantity without quality, it is not possible to have quality without quantity in relation to the characteristics of the institution.

The library collection should be continually evaluated against standard bibliographies and evolving institutional requirements for purposes of adding new titles and identifying for withdrawal those titles which have outlived their usefulness. No titles should be retained for which a clear purpose is not evident in terms of academic programs or extracurricular enrichment.

The best way to preserve or improve quality in a college library collection is to adhere to rigorous standards of discrimination in the selection of materials to be added, whether as purchases or gifts. The collection should contain a substantial portion of the titles listed in standard bibliographies for the curricular areas of the institution and for supporting general fields of knowledge. Subject lists for college libraries have been prepared by several learned associations, while general bibliographies such as *Books for College Libraries* are especially useful for identifying important retrospective titles. A majority of the appropriate, current publications reviewed in scholarly journals and in reviewing media such as *Choice* or *Library Journal* should be acquired. Careful attention should also be given to standard works of reference and to bibliographical tools which describe the broad range of information sources.

Institutional needs for periodical holdings vary widely. In general it is good practice to consider owning any title that is needed more than five times per year. Several good lists have been prepared of periodical titles appropriate or necessary for college collections. Katz's *Magazines for Libraries* describes several thousand titles and is useful in this regard. It may not be necessary to subscribe to certain less frequently used titles if they are available at another library nearby, or if needed articles may be quickly procured through a reliable delivery system or by electronic means.

While it is important that a library have in its collection the quantity of materials called for in Formula A, its resources ought to be augmented whenever appropriate with external collections and services. A library that meets part of its responsibilities in this way must ensure that such activities do not weaken a continuing commitment to develop its own holdings. There is no substitute for a strong, immediately accessible collection. Moreover, once a collection has attained the size called for by this formula, its usefulness will soon diminish if new materials are not acquired. Libraries with collections that are significantly below the size recommended in Formula A should maintain a 5 percent growth rate until they can claim a grade of A. (see standard 2.2). Those that meet or exceed the criteria for a grade of A may find it unrealistic or unnecessary to sustain a growth rate as high as 5 percent. Although the scope and content of the collection is ultimately the responsibility of the librarians, this responsibility can be best fulfilled by developing clear selection policies in cooperation with the classroom faculty. Moreover, the classroom faculty should be encouraged to participate in the selection of new titles for the collection.

2.2 The amount of print materia to be provided by the library shall be determined by a formula (see Formula A) which takes into account the nature and extent of the academic program of the institution, its enrollment, and the size of the classroom faculty.

Commentary.

A. Print resources. A strong core collection of print materials, augmented by specific allowances for enrollment, faculty size, and curricular offerings, is an indispensable requirement for the library of any college. The degree to which a library meets this requirement may be calculated with Formula A.

B.   Audiovisual resources. The range, extent, and configuration of nonprint resources and services in college libraries varies widely according to institutional needs and characteristics. Audiovisual holdings may be counted as volume unit equivalents and this number should be added to that for print volumes and volume-equivalents in measuring a library's collection against Formula A. If some or all of this material is housed in an administratively separate media center or audiovisual facility, it may be included in the grade determination if properly organized for use and readily accessible to the college community.

C. Determination of grade. The degree to which a library provides its users with materials is graded by comparing the total holdings of volumes and volume-equivalents with the results of Formula A calculations.

Standard 3: Organization of Materials
3. Library collections shall be organized by nationally approved conventions and arranged for efficient retrieval at time of need.
Commentary. The acquisition of library materials comprises only part of the task of providing access to them. Collections should be indexed and arranged systematically to assure efficient identification and retrieval.
3.1 There shall be a comprehensive catalog of the library's holdings that permits identification of items, regardless of format or location, by author, title, and by subject, as appropriate.
Commentary. The catalog should be comprehensive and provide bibliographic access to materials in all formats owned by the library. This can best be accomplished through the development of a catalog with items entered in accord with established national or international bibliographical conventions, such as rules for entry, descriptive cataloging, filing, classification, and subject headings.

Opportunities of several kinds exist for the cooperative development of the library's catalog. These include the use of cataloging information produced by the Library of Congress and the various bibliographic utilities. It may also include the compilation by a number of libraries of a shared catalog. Catalogs should be subject to appropriate editing to keep them abreast of modern technology, contemporary practice, and changing national and international information standards such as MARC, AACR2, and NISO.
3.1.1 The catalog shall be in a format that can be consulted by a number of users concurrently.
Commentary. A public catalog in any format can satisfy this standard if it is so arranged that the library's users normally encounter no delay in gaining access to it.
3.1.2 In addition to the catalog there shall also be requisite subordinate files to provide bibliographic control and access to all library materials.
Commentary. Proper organization of the collections requires the maintenance of a number of subordinate files, such as authority files, shelf lists, and complementary catalogs, such as serial holdings

records, as appropriate. Information contained in these files should also be made accessible through indexes in printed or computer based format.

3.2   Library materials shall be arranged to provide maximum accessibility to all users. Certain categories of materials may be segregated by form or for convenience.

Commentary. Materials should be arranged so that related information can be easily consulted. Some materials, such as rarities, manuscripts, or archives may be segregated for purposes of security or presentation. Materials in exceptionally active use, reference works, and microforms are examples of resources that may be awkward to integrate physically because of format and may need to be segregated from the main collection. Fragmentation of the collection should be avoided whenever possible, however, with the bulk of the collections shelved by subject in open stack areas to permit and encourage browsing.

3.3 Materials placed in storage facilities shall be readily accessible to users.

Commentary. Many libraries or groups of libraries have developed storage facilities for low-use materials such as sets and backruns of journals. These facilities may be situated on camps or in remote locations. The materials housed in these facilities should be easily identifiable and readily available for use in a timely fashion. If direct user access is not possible, a rapid retrieval system should be provided.

Standard 4: Staff

4.   The staff shall be of adequate size and quality to meet the library's need for services, programs, and collection organization.

Commentary. The college library shall need a staff composed of qualified librarians, skilled support personnel, and student assistants to carry out its stated objectives.

4.1   Librarians, including the director, shall have a graduate degree from an ALA-accredited program, shall be responsible for duties of a professional nature, and shall participate in professional activities.

Commentary.   The librarian has acquired through education in a graduate school of library and information science an understanding of the principles and theories of selection, acquisition, organization, interpretation, and administration of library resources. It should be noted that the MLS is regarded as a terminal professional degree by ALA and ACRL. Moreover, developments in computer and information technology have had a major impact on librarianship, requiring that librarians be well informed in this constantly developing area.

Librarians shall be assigned responsibilities which are appropriate to their education and which encourage the ongoing development of professional competencies. Participation in library and other professional activities on and off campus is also necessary to further personal development.

4.2 Librarians shall be organized as a separate academic unit such as a department or a school. They shall administer themselves in accord with ACRL's "Standards for Faculty Status for College and University Librarians" and institutional policies and guidelines

Commentary. Librarians comprise the faculty of the library and should organize, administer, and govern themselves accordingly. The status, responsibilities, perquisites, and governance of the library faculty shall be fully organized and supported by the parent institution.

4.3 The number of librarians required shall be determined by a formula (see Formula B) and shall further take into consideration the goals and services of the library, programs, degrees offered, institutional enrollment, size of faculty and staff, and auxiliary programs.

Commentary. Formula B is based on student enrollment, collection size, and annual change in size of the collection. Other factors to be considered in determining staff size are services and programs, degrees offered, size of faculty and staff, and auxiliary programs. Examples of services and programs include reference and information services, bibliographic instruction, computer based services, collection development, and collection organization. In addition, auxiliary programs, e.g., extension, community, and continuing education, as well as size and configuration of facilities and hours of service, are factors to be considered for determining adequate staff size.

4.4 The support staff and student assistants shall be assigned responsibilities appropriate to their qualification, training, experience, and capabilities. The support staff shall be no less than 65 percent of the total library staff, not including student assistants.

Commentary. Full-time and part-time support staff carry out a wide variety of paraprofessional, technical, and clerical responsibilities. A productive working relationship between librarians and support staff is an essential ingredient in the successful operation of the library. In addition student assistants provide meaningful support in accomplishing many library tasks.

4.5 Library policies and procedures concerning staff shall be in accord with institutional guidelines and sound personnel management.

Commentary. The staff represents one of the library's most important assets in support of the instructional program of the college. Its management must be based upon sound, contemporary practices and procedures consistent with the goals and purposes of the institution, including the following:

1.   Recruitment methods should be based upon a careful definition of positions to be filled and objective evaluation of credentials and qualification.
2.   Written procedures should be developed in accordance with ACRL and institutional guidelines, and followed in matters of appointment, promotion, tenure dismissal and appeal.
3.   Every staff member should be informed in writing as to the scope of his/her responsibilities.
4.   Rates of pay and benefits of library staff should be equivalent to other positions on campus requiring comparable backgrounds.
5.   There should be a structured program for orientation and training of new staff members, and career development should be provided for all staff.
6.   Supervisory staff should be selected on a basis of job knowledge, experience, and human relations skills.
7.   Procedures should be maintained for periodic review of staff performance and for recognition of achievement. See relevant ACRL documents listed in the bibliography.

Standard 5: Services

5.   The library shall establish, promote, and maintain a range and quality of services that will support the academic program of the institution and encourage optimal library use.

Commentary. The primary purpose of the college library is to promote and support the academic program of the parent institution. Services should be developed for and made available to all members of the academic community, including persons with disabilities and nontraditional students. The successful fulfillment of this purpose will require that librarians work closely with classroom faculty to gain from them a clear understanding of their educational objectives and teaching methods and to communicate to them an understanding of the services and resources which the library can offer. While research skill and ease of access to materials will both serve and encourage library use, the primary motivation for students to use the library originates with the instructional method used in the classroom. Thus, close cooperation between librarians and classroom faculty is essential. Such cooperation must result from planned and structured activity and requires that librarians participate in the academic planning councils of the institution. They should assist classroom faculty in appraising the actual and potential library resources available, work closely with them in developing library services to support their instructional activities, and keep them informed of library capabilities.

5.1 The library shall provide information and instruction to the user through a variety of techniques to meet differing needs. These shall include but not be limited to a variety of professional reference services and bibliographic instruction programs designed to teach users how to take full advantage of the resources available to them.

Commentary. A fundamental responsibility of a college library is to provide instruction in the most effective and efficient use of its materials. Bibliographic instruction and orientation may be given at many levels of sophistication and may use a variety of methods and materials, including course-related instruction, separate courses (with or without credit), and group or individualized instruction.

Of equal importance is traditional reference service wherein individual users are guided by librarians in their appraisal of the range and extent of the library and information resources available to them for learning and research. Professional services are optimally available all hours the library is open. Use patterns should be studied to determine those times when the absence of professional assistance would be least detrimental. The third major form of information service is the delivery of information itself. Although obviously inappropriate in the case of student searches which are purposeful segments of classroom assignment, the actual delivery of information—as distinct from guidance to it—is a reasonable library service in almost all other conceivable situations.

Many of the services suggested in this commentary can be provided or enhanced by access to computerized forms of information retrieval. Many information sources are available only in computerized format, and every effort should be made to provide access to them. Services may be provided in person or through other means such as videocassette, computer programs, or other appropriately prepared programs.

5.2 Library materials of all types and formats that can be used outside the library shall be circulated to qualified users under equitable policies without jeopardizing their presentation or availability to others.

Commentary. Circulation of library materials should be determined by local conditions which will include size of the collection, the number of copies, and the extent of the user community. Every effort should be made to circulate materials of all formats that can be used outside the library without undue risk to their presentation. Circulation should be for as long a period as is reasonable without jeopardizing access to materials by other qualified users. This overall goal may prompt some institutions to establish variant or unique loan periods for different titles or classes of titles. Whatever loan policy is used, it should be equitable and uniformly administered to all qualified categories of users. The accessibility of materials can also be extended through provisions of inexpensive means of photocopying within the laws regarding copyright.

5.3 Interlibrary loan activities, cooperative programs, and utilization of commercial services shall be encouraged for the purpose of extending and increasing services and resources.

Commentary.   The rapid growth of information sources, the availability of a variety of automation services, and the development of new technologies continue to impact a library's ability to provide services and resources. Cooperation with other institutions, and particularly with multitype library organizations, often becomes a necessity. This involves not only receiving, but also a willingness to give or share, on the part of each library. Formal reciprocal agreements, according to ALA codes, may need to be developed. Access to materials should be by the most efficient and rapid method possible, incorporating such measures as delivery services, rental services, and electronic mail in addition to, or in place of, traditional forms of delivery. The extent of resource sharing through ILL, cooperative arrangements, and other delivery methods should be recognized in any assessment of the ability of a library to supply its users with needed materials.

5.4   The hours of access to the library shall be consistent with reasonable demand.

Commentary. The number of hours per week that library services are available will vary as a reflection of reasonable local need. During peak hours of operation the users deserve competent, professional service. However, in some institutions users may need access to study facilities and to the collections, in whole or in part, during more hours of the week than they may need personal assistance. In any case, the high value of the library's facilities, collections, associated materials, and equipment dictates that responsible personnel be on duty at all times.

5.5 Where academic programs are offered at off-campus sites, library services shall be provided in accord with ACRL's "Guidelines for Extended Campus Library Services".

Commentary. Special library problems exist for colleges that provide off-campus institutional programs. Students in such programs must be provided with library services in accord with ACRL's "Guidelines for Extended Campus Library Services." These guidelines suggest that such services be financed on a regular basis, that a librarian be specifically charged with the delivery of such services, that the library implications of such programs be considered before program approval, and that courses so taught encourage library use. Services should be designed to meet the different information and bibliographic needs of these users.

Standard 6: Facilities

6. The library building shall provide well planned, secure and adequate housing for its collections and personnel, secure space for users and staff, and space for the provision of services and programs.

Commentary. Successful library service presupposes an adequate library building. Although the type of building will depend upon the character and purposes of the institution, it should in all cases be functional, providing secure facilities for accommodating the library's personnel and resources, sufficient space for their administration and maintenance, and secure and comfortable reading and study areas for users. A new library building should represent a coordinated planning effort involving the library director and staff, the college administration, campus constituents, and the architect, with the director responsible for the preparation of the building program.

The needs of persons with disabilities should receive special attention and should be provided for in compliance with the Architectural Barriers Act of 1968 (Public Law 93-480) and the Rehabilitation Act of 1973, Section 504 (Public Law 93-516), and their amendments; and the Americans with Disabilities Act of 1990 (Public Law 101-336).

Particular consideration must be given to any present or future requirements for equipment associated with automated systems or other applications of library technology. Among these might be provision for new wiring, cabling, special climate control, and maximum flexibility in the use of space. Consideration should also be given to load-bearing requirements for compact shelving and the housing of mixed formats including microforms.

6.1 The size of the library building shall be determined by a formula (see Formula C) which takes into account the enrollment of the college, the extent and nature of its collections, and the size of the staff.

6.2 In designing or managing a library building, the functionality of floor plan and the use of space shall be the paramount concern.

Commentary. The quality of a building is measured by such characteristics as the utility and comfort of its study and office areas, the design and durability of its furniture and equipment, the functional interrelationships of its service and work areas, and the ease and economy with which it can be operated and used.

6.3 Except in certain circumstances, the college library's collections and services shall be administered within a single structure.

Commentary. Decentralized library facilities in a college have some virtues, and they present some difficulties. Primary among their virtues is the convenience to the offices or laboratories of some of the classroom faculty. Primary among their weaknesses is the resulting fragmentation of the unit of knowledge, the relative isolation of a branch library from most users, potential problems of staffing and security, and the cost of maintaining certain duplicate services or functions. When decentralized library facilities are being considered, these costs and benefits must be carefully compared. In general, experience has shown that decentralized library facilities may not be in the best academic or economic interest of a college.

Standard 7: Administration

Matters pertaining to college library administration are treated in several other standards. Matters of personnel administration, for example, are discussed in standard 4, and fiscal administration in standard 8. Some important aspects of library management, however, must be considered apart from the other standards.

7. The college library shall be administered in a manner which permits and encourages the fullest and most effective use of available library resources.

Commentary. The function of a library administrator is to direct and coordinate the components of the library—its staff, services, collections, buildings, and external relations. Each component contributes effectively and imaginatively to the mission of the library.

7.1 The statutory or legal foundation for the library's activities shall be recognized in writing.

Commentary. In order for the library to function effectively, there must be an articulated understanding within the college as to the statutory or legal basis under which the library operates. This may be a college bylaw, a trustee minute, or a public law which shows the responsibility and flow of authority under which the library is empowered to act.

7.2 The library director shall be an officer of the college and shall report to the president or the chief academic officer of the institution.

Commentary. For the closest coordination of library activities with the instructional program, the library director should report to either the president or the chief officer in charge of the academic affairs of the institution.

7.2.1 The responsibilities and authority of the library director and procedures for appointment shall be defined in writing.

Commentary. There should be a document defining the responsibility and authority vested in the library director. This document may also be statutorily based and should spell out, in addition to the scope and nature of the director's duties and powers, the procedures for appointment.

7.3 There shall be a standing advisory committee comprised of students and members of the classroom faculty which shall serve as a channel of formal communication between the library and its user community.

Commentary. This committee—of which the library director should be an ex-officio member—should be used to convey both an awareness to the library of its users' concerns, perceptions, and needs, and an understanding to users of the library's objectives and capabilities. The charge to the committee should be specific and in writing.

7.4 The library shall maintain written policies and procedures manuals covering internal library governance and operation activities.

Commentary. Written policies and procedures manuals are required for good management, uniformity, and consistency of action. They also aid in training staff and contribute to public understanding.

7.4.1 The library shall maintain a systematic and continuous program for evaluating its performance, for informing the community of its accomplishments, and for identifying needed improvement.

Commentary. The library director, in conjunction with the staff, should develop a program for evaluating the library's performance. Objectives developed in accordance with the goals of the institution should play a major part in this evaluation program. Statistics should be maintained for use in reports, to demonstrate trends, and in performance evaluation. At the discretion of the library director and in accordance with institutional requirements, the statistics may include data related to input measures, output measures, and/or assessment. In addition, the library director and staff members should seek the assistance of the standing library advisory committee and other representatives of the community.

7.5 The library shall be administered in accord with the spirit of the ALA "Library Bill of Rights".

Commentary. College libraries should be impervious to the pleasures or efforts of any special interest groups or individuals to shape their collections and services. This principle, first postulated by the American Library Association in 1939 as the "Library Bill of Rights" (amended 1948, 1961, 1967, and 1980 by the ALA Council), should govern the administration of every college library and be given the full protection of the parent institution.

Standard 8: Budget

8.　The library director shall have the responsibility for preparing, defending, and administering the library budget in accord with agreed upon objectives.

Commentary. The library's budget is a function of program planning and defines the library's objectives in fiscal terms. The objectives formulated under standard 1 should constitute the base upon which the library's budget is developed.

8.1　The library's annual authorized expenditures shall be at least 6 percent of the total institutional expenditure for educational and general purposes. The library should receive its appropriation at the beginning of the budget cycle for the institution.

Commentary. The degree to which the college is able to fund the library in accord with institutional objectives is reflected in the relationship of the library appropriation to the total educational and general budget of the college. It is recommended that library budgets, exclusive of capital costs and the costs of physical maintenance, not fall below 6 percent of the college's total educational and general expenditures if the library is to sustain the range of programs required by the institution and meet appropriate institutional objectives. This percentage should be greater if the library is attempting to overcome past deficiencies, or to meet the needs of new academic programs. The 6 percent figure is intended to include support for separately established professional libraries, providing the budget for those schools is incorporated into that of the college or university.

Factors which should be considered in formulating a library's budget requirements are the following:

1. The scope, nature, and level of the college curriculum;
2. Instructional methods used, especially as they relate to independent study;
3. The adequacy of existing collections and the publishing rate in fields pertinent to the curriculum;

4. The size, or anticipated size, of the student body and classroom faculty;
5. The adequacy and availability of other library resources;
6. The range of services offered by the library, for example, the number of service points maintained, the number of hours per week that service is provided, the level of bibliographic instruction, online services, etc.;
7. The extent of automation of operations and services, with attendant costs;
8. The extent to which the library already meets the *Standards for College Libraries*.

8.1.1 The library's appropriation shall be augmented above the 6 percent level depending on the extent to which it bears responsibility for acquiring, processing, and servicing audiovisual material, and microcomputer resources.

Commentary. It is difficult for any academic library that has not traditionally been purchasing microcomputer and audiovisual materials to accommodate such purchases without some budgetary increase. The level of expenditure depends on whether or not the institution has an audiovisual center separate from the library that acquires and maintains both audiovisual materials and hardware as well as a computer center that absorbs all costs related too microcomputer resources, even those included in the library.

8.2 The library director shall have the sole authority to apportion funds and initiate expenditures within the library budget and in accord with institutional policy.

Commentary. Procedures for the preparation and defense of budget estimates, policies on budget approval, and regulation concerning accounting and expenditures vary from one institution to another. The library director must know and conform to local procedure. Sound practices of planning and local control require that the director have sole responsibility and authority for allocation—and within college policy, the reallocation—of the library budget and the initiation of expenditures against it. Depending on local factors, between 35 percent and 45 percent of the library's budget is normally allocated to acquisition of resources; between 50 percent and 60 percent is expended for personnel.

8.3 Any revenues generated by the library from fees and charges such as fines, payments for lost or damaged materials, and from the sale of duplicate or unneeded items should be retained by the library for support of collections and services.

Commentary. In some jurisdictions, local laws place restrictions on this concept. However, it is acceptable practice in many areas now, and the committee would like to see the practice encouraged.

8.4 The library should maintain internal accounts for approving its invoices for payment, monitoring its encumbrance, and evaluating flow of its expenditures.

Commentary. Periodic reports are necessary and provide an accurate account of the funds allocated to the library. They should be current and made accessible for fiscal accountability.

Formula A: Collections

1.	Basic collection	85,000 vols.
2.	Allowance per FTE faculty member	100 vols.
3.	Allowance per FTE student	15 vols.
4.	Allowance per undergraduate major or minor field*	350 vols.
5.	Allowance per master's field, when no higher degree is offered in the field*	6,000 vols.
6.	Allowance per master's field, when a higher degree is offered in the field*	3,000 vols.
7.	Allowance per sixth year specialist degree field*	6,000 vols.
8.	Allowance per doctoral field*	25,000 vols.

These figures are to be calculated cumulatively. A "volume" is defined as a physical unit of work which has been printed or otherwise reproduced, typewritten, or handwritten, contained in one binding or portfolio, hardbound or paperbound, which has been cataloged, classified, or otherwise prepared for use. Microform holdings should be converted to volume-equivalents, whether by actual count or by an averaging formula which considers each reel of microfilm, or ten pieces of any other microform, as one volume-equivalent. Audiovisual materials include videocassettes, films, and videodisks (1 item = 1 VUE, volume unit equivalent), sound recordings, filmstrips, loops, slide tape sets, graphic materials including maps, and computer software packages (1 item = 1 VUE), and slides (50 slides = 1 VUE). This approach may be adapted to other nonprint formats.

*For an example of a list of fields see Robert Morgan's *Classification of Instructional Programs* (NCES, 1990).

Libraries that can provide 90 to 100 percent of as many volumes as are called for in Formula A shall be graded A in terms of library resources;

from 75 to 89 percent shall be graded B; 60 to 74 percent, shall be graded C; and 5 to 59 percent shall be graded D.

Formula B: Librarians

For each 500, or fraction thereof, FTE students up to 10,000	1 librarian
For each 1,000, or fraction thereof, FTE students above 10,000	1 librarian
For each 100,000 volumes, or fraction thereof, in the collection	1 librarian
For each 5,000 volumes, or fraction thereof, added and/or withdrawn per year	1 librarian

Enrollment, collection size, and growth of collection determine the number of librarians required by the college. These figures are to be calculated cumulatively. Libraries which provide 90-100 percent of these formula requirements can, provided they are supported by sufficient other staff members as described in standard 4.4, consider themselves at the A level in terms of staff size; those that provide 75 to 89 percent of these requirements may rate themselves as B; those with 60 to 74 percent of requirements qualify for a C; and those with 50 to 59 percent of requirements warrant a D. This formula does not include campuswide media, archives, or academic computing services when administered by the library. Those units require additional personnel.

Supplemental staffing factors to be considered

Organizational and Institutional
The individual library's organization and institutional factors also influence its staffing needs. Additional factors to be considered are as follows:

Library   Institutional

- Services and programs   • Degrees offered
- Size and configuration of facilities • Size of faculty and staff
- Hours of service   • Auxiliary programs

Examples of services and programs   Examples of institutional factors

- Reference and information   • Undergraduate programs
- Bibliographic instruction   • Graduate programs
- Computer based services   • Research
- Collection development   • Community
- Collection organization   • Continuing education
- Archives
- Audiovisual services

Formula C: Facilities

The size of the college library building shall be calculated on the basis of a formula which takes into consideration the size of the student body, the size of the staff and its space requirements, and the number of volumes in the collection. To the result of this calculation must be added such space as may be required to house and service nonprint materials and microforms, to provide bibliographic instruction to groups, and to accommodate equipment and services associated with various forms of library technology. The formula may need to be adjusted in accordance with local interpretation and application of the requirements of the Americans with Disabilities Act of 1990.

a) *Space for users.* The seating requirement for a library of a college when less than 50 percent of the FTE enrollment resides on campus shall be one for each five students. That for the library of a typical residential college shall be one for each four FTE students. Each study station shall be assumed to require twenty five to thirty five square feet for floor space, depending upon its function.

b) *Space for books.* The space allocated for books shall be adequate to accommodate a convenient and orderly distribution of the collection according to the classification system(s) in use, and should include space for growth. Gross space requirements may be estimated according to the following formula:

	Square Feet/Volume
For the first 150,000 volumes	0.10

For the next 150,000 volumes	0.09
For the next 300,000 volumes	0.08
For holdings above 600,000 volumes	0.07

c) *Space for staff.* Space required for staff offices, service and work areas, catalogs, files and equipment shall be approximately one-eighth of the sum of the space needed for books and users as calculated under (a) and (b) above.

This formula indicates the net assignable area required by a library if it is to fulfill its mission with maximum effectiveness. "Net assignable area" is the sum of all areas (measured in square feet) on all floors of a building, assignable to, or useful for, library functions or purposes. (For an explanation of this definition see *Measurement and Comparison of Physical Facilities for Libraries*, ALA, 1970.

Libraries which provide 90 to 100 percent of the *net* assignable area called for by the formula shall be graded A in terms of space; 75 to 89 percent shall be graded B; 60 to 74 percent shall be graded C; and 50 to 59 percent shall be graded D.

BIBLIOGRAPHY

ACRL. "Guidelines for Audiovisual Services in Academic Libraries." *C&RL News* 48 (October 1987): 533-36.

ACRL. "Guidelines for Extended Campus Library Service." *C&RL News* 51 (April 1990): 353-55.

ACRL. "Model Statement for the Screening and Appointment of Academic Librarians Using a Search Committee." *C&RL News* 53 (November 1992): 642-45.

ACRL. "Model Statement of Criteria and Procedures for Appointment, Promotion in Academic Rank, and Tenure for College and University Librarians." *C&RL News* 48 (May 1987): 247-54.

ACRL. " Model Statement of Objectives for Academic Bibliographic Instruction." *C&RL News* 48 (May 1987): 256-61.

ACRL. "Standards for Community, Junior and Technical College Learning Resources Programs." *C&RL News* 51 (September 1990): 757-67.

ACRL. "Standards for Faculty Status for College and University Librarians *C&RL News* 53 (May 1974): 317-18.

ACRL. "Standards for University Libraries: Evaluation of Performance" *C&RL News* 50 (September 1989): 679-81.

ACRL. "Statement on the Terminal Professional Degree for Academic Librarians." Chicago: ALA/ACRL, 1975.

ALA Ad Hoc Committee on the Physical Facilities of Libraries. *Measurement and Comparison of Physical Facilities for Libraries*. Chicago: ALA, 1970.

ALA. "Library Bill of Rights" (ALA Policy Manual, Section 53.1) In
ALA *Handbook of Organization 1993-1994*. Chicago, ALA, 1993, p.H147.

ALA. "Library Education and Personnel Utilization: A Statement of Policy."
Adopted by ALA Council. Chicago: ALA/OLPR, 1970.

ALA, RSDA/FLA. *National Interlibrary Loan Code, 1980; International
Lending Principles and Guidelines,* 1978. Chicago: ALA, 1982.

Carpenter, Ray L. "College Libraries: A Comparative Analysis in Terms of the
ACRL Standards." *College and Research Libraries* 42 (January 1981): 7-
18.

Coleman, Paul and Ada Jarred. "Regional Accreditation Criteria and the
Standards for College Libraries: The Informal Role of Quantitative Input
Measures for Libraries in Accreditation." *Journal of Academic
Librarianship* 20 (November 1994):273 - 84.

Hardesty, Larry, and Stella Bentley. *The Use and Effectiveness of the 1975
Standards for College Libraries: A Survey of College Library Directors*
(1981). Unpublished paper.

Kaser, David. "Standards for College Libraries." *Library Trends* 31:1 (Summer
1982): 7-19.

Kroll, Susan, ed. *Academic Status: Statements and Resources,* 2nd ed.
Chicago: ACRL/ALA, 1994.

Leach, Ronald G. and Judith E. Tribble. "Electronic Document Delivery: New
Options for Libraries." *Journal of Academic Librarianship* 18 (January
1993): 359-64.

Matier, Michael, and C. Clinton Sidle. "What Size Libraries for 2010 *Planning
for Higher Education* 21 (Summer 1993): 9-15.

Morgan, Robert L. *Classification of Instructional Programs,* 1990 edition
Washington, D.C.: National Center for Educational Statistics, 1991.

Sacks, Patricia Ann, and Sara Lou Whildin. *Preparing for Accreditation: A
Handbook for Academic Librarians* .Chicago: ALA, 1993.

Stueart, Robert D., and Barbara Moran. "Mission, Goals and Objectives." In
*Library and Information Center Management,*4 th ed. Englewood, Colo:
Libraries Unlimited, 1993, pp. 43-45.

U.S. Code. 1-810. "Act for the General Revision of the Copyright Law."
October 9, 1976. Public Law 94-553, 90 Stat. 2541.

Walch, David B., "The 1986 College Library Standards: Application and
Utilization." *College and Research Libraries* 54 (May 1993): 217-26.

(Ed. note: *Committee members who worked on the 1995 edition are: Diane C.
Parker, chair, Western Washington University; Barbara Bryan, Fairfield
University; Paul Coleman, Adrian College; Jan Fennell, Georgia College,
Milledgeville; Dalia Hagan, St. Martins College; Ada Jarred, Northwestern
State University of Louisiana; Eric Kidwell, Huntingdon College; Grady
Morein, University of West Florida: and Norma Yueh, Ramapo College of New
Jersey.*)

INDEX

ABOUT THE AUTHORS

Caroline M. Coughlin (A.B., Mercy College, M.Ln., Emory University, Ph.D., Rutgers University) is a part-time faculty member at the School of Communication, Information and Library Studies at Rutgers University and a library consultant. From 1978 to 1994 she was employed at the Drew University Library in Madison, N.J. where she served as Assistant Director, then Director and Associate Professor of Research and Bibliography. She has taught at the library schools of Emory University, University of Alabama, Simmons College, University of Wales, University of Washington and at the Continuing Education Centre in Tampere, Finland. Dr. Coughlin is active in national and regional library associations and has been elected Member-at-Large, ALA Council, Director (for Associate Members), Center for Research Libraries Board, and President, College and University Section, New Jersey Library Association. She is a member of the 1988 class of Senior Fellows at the Graduate School of Library and Information Science, University of California at Los Angeles and the 1993 recipient of both the Distinguished Service Award and the Research Award of the College and University Section of the New Jersey Library Association. She regularly serves on accreditation visiting teams for the Middle States Association, on evaluation panels for federal grant applications and as a consultant to academic libraries and speaker on library management. She has published articles in professional journals, edited a book of readings, *Recurring Library Issues* (Scarecrow, 1979) and co-authored the fifth edition of *Lyle's Administration of the College Library* (Scarecrow, 1992) with Alice Gertzog.

Alice Gertzog is a graduate of Antioch College. She earned her MLS degree from Catholic University of Washington, D.C. and her Ph.D. from Rutgers University. Dr. Gertzog has been a librarian at the University of North Carolina, Yale University and New Haven College. In addition, she has worked in special and public libraries, has been a library consultant, and has taught at the Rutgers University School of Communication, Information and Library Studies. She has published articles in professional journals, authored *Case Studies in College Library Administration* (Scarecrow, 1992) as a companion volume to *Lyle's Administration of the College Library* (Scarecrow, 1992) which she co-authored with Caroline M. Coughlin. In 1994 she co-authored (with Edwin Beckerman) *Administration of the Public Library* (Scarecrow). She is the recipient of the 1993 Research Award of the College and University Section of the New Jersey Library Association.